REDEEMING MODERN MARRIAGE

A Primer for Navigating the Headwinds Facing the Family Unit

By
Innocent N. Barasa
M.Div., D.Min(c)

2nd Printing

ISBN: 978-1-949565-12-6

Printed in the U.S.A. by
Smith Printing Company, LLC
Ramsey, MN 55303
(800) 416-9099 • www.smithprinting.com
Printed in the USA

TABLE OF CONTENTS

PREFACE

REDEEMING MODERN MARRIAGES: *A Primer for Navigating the Headwinds Facing the Family Unit* is not an in-depth scholarly treatise with research and data that interrogates the mechanics and praxis of modern marriages; instead, it is a biblical treatment that focuses on the salient and pertinent issues gravitating about the institution and theology of marriage in our modern societies. We give specific attention to the challenges facing marriages in the North American landscape and a cursory glance at the African narrative as well. Evidence on the ground shows a dire situation in which many families are agonizing over marriages that have turned sour and loveless. Nevertheless, on the positive side, overall divorce numbers seem to be coming down in the latest national statistics, but a worrying trend is emerging, with the number of new marriages continuing to dwindle over the years since 2000. This could mean, for some reason, marriage is becoming more unattractive to many single people, whose number seems to be constantly soaring.

Whereas it is not our intention to investigate why more and more unmarried people are shunning marriage, we believe the reasons responsible for divorce form part of the reasons why marriage is being avoided, with many choosing to remain single. Marriage counselors, pastors, and therapists have offered their very best to address these growing concerns, but the situation has not changed much. This book is an attempt to trace and locate where the rain started beating us in our marriages.

Nonetheless, what has remained unmistakable are the millions of complaints in marriage on domestic abuse, infidelity, money, gender roles, submission, headship, bossing, and more, which explain the genesis of the simmering tension in the relationships within our societies today.

In this primer, we have tried to isolate the most notorious areas where couples contend with strong marital headwinds and a raft of prescriptive, biblical, emotional, and social interventions to stabilize the floundering relationships in our society. Suggestions on how to increase the capacity for both newlyweds and older couples to successfully navigate through the headwinds of the lifelong marital journey have been put forward. The book traces the foundation of marriage to its biblical antecedents and juxtaposes the biblical fabric vis-à-vis the American and African narratives from cultural marital standpoints. The juxtaposition will help to elucidate deviations from the prototypical normative marriage in the Garden, which was solemnized and flagged off by the pioneer officiant, even the Creator Himself. When God initiated and called marriage into existence, He wanted it to be holy and honorable before Him because it mirrors the relationship between the Christ and the Church - in the aspect of the bond of love and selfless giving that is meant to undergird it.

When we refer to the scriptures to get insights into God's original design, many people could argue that the Bible cannot give all of the answers about marriage because Scripture is not a marriage handbook. However, we have been intentional in referring to the Scriptures multiple times because we believe that way, we can better understand the algorithm of marriage, which will help us stem the turmoil experienced in the family unit today. We believe marriage is a God idea. Therefore, we shall be better off going back to His counsel if we have to draft a roadmap for enduring and God-honoring marriage relationships. Marriage occupies a special place in His Creation.

The ecclesiastical relationship between Christ and the Church is a metaphor for the relationship between a husband and a wife. This metaphor sets marriage apart as God's divine way for self-disclosure to His creation. Therefore, the character of God should be revealed in all marriages. The motif of God's covenant faithfulness plays out in its entirety in any healthy marriage relationship, and it is a central indicator for any functional marriage.

DEDICATION

This book is dedicated to my late wife,
Grace Kerubo Nyagitari, who went to be with the
Lord on April 10th, 2013, after a gallant battle with cancer.
For us, to live is Christ; to die is even gain.
To God be the glory. Amen.

INTRODUCTION

Marriage could perhaps be the most misconstrued phenomenon in world societies today. Different communities assign different meanings and lay different expectations and emphases on marriage. Confusion as to who should marry who juts its head amidst the melee of identity crises, and there is a deviation from the heterosexual biblical imperative. Selling the commodity of marriage in a world espousing individualism as its watermark for modernity is increasingly becoming a lackluster business. A marriage relationship is seen by many in our modern societies as confining, limiting, and a jail term for which every freedom-loving "inmate" should engage the services of the best attorneys to secure "parole." Some dismiss marriage as being boring and burdensome.

The good news is that the most current statistics show that the divorce rate is not as alarming as previously thought. According to *National Vital Statistics Reports - USA*, the number of divorces and annulments between 2000 and 2017 has been declining over the years, with a rate of 4.0 divorces out of a population of 1000 in the year 2000, to a rate of 2.9 divorces out of a population of 1000 in the year 2017. However, the provisional number of marriages and the marriage rate within this period has been declining from 8.2 marriages per every 1000 in the year 2000 to a rate of 6.9 for every

1000 people in the year 2017. This is despite the fact that there was a significant increase in population between those periods.[1]

The above statistics are comforting on the one hand, as divorce is slowing down, but also troubling on the other, as marriages have been declining in recent years, even though the population has been increasing. The reasons for the aversion to entering marriage relationships might not necessarily be economical. During this period, even when the economy was doing well and the unemployment rate was low, a decline in the number of new marriages was, unfortunately, a glaring time bomb. This is a pointer to the fact that there could be inherent problems within a marriage, requiring new approaches and techniques to sort out the mess responsible for the apparent change of dynamics.

On the flip side, an interesting scenario emerges when the phrase "marriage relationship" evokes different meanings in different cultures. It is not unusual in the American culture to find that a couple, which could be referred to as husband and wife in Africa, is simply referred to as boyfriend and girlfriend. Alternatively, the American guy would say, "she is a mother to my kids" instead of "my wife," while a lady could say, "he is a father to my kids," instead of "my husband." In Africa, when a man and woman live together under one roof, with or without children, the arrangement is socially recognized and accorded the respect of a marriage relationship. This girlfriend/boyfriend kind of arrangement doesn't apply in an African cultural setting. A question that cannot fail to be asked is why many people, especially men, see using the title of husband/wife as anathema and prefer boyfriend/girlfriend instead, especially in North America. Perhaps the legal and

[1] "National marriage and divorce rate trends," CDC, https://www.cdc.gov/nchs/data/dvs/national-marriage-divorce-rates-00-17.pdf

social implications involved in the assumption of these statuses justify this aversion. Along with that, while in some communities, divorce is a negative phenomenon laden with stigma and scorn, in others, the same word elicits hilarious feelings of being enlightened, liberated, and knowledgeable about personal freedoms, rights, and obligations—without an iota of stigma whatsoever.

Keeping that aside, the expectations laid on marriage are diverse, often unrealistic, and unattainable, resulting in thousands of separations and divorce cases, particularly here in the West. Many are those who come into a marriage with fantasies of a utopian nature. They come expecting joy and happiness without limits, which they whimsically hope will come spontaneously. Some imagine finding untold riches and wealth in marriage, while others hope to sire and bear children as beautiful as the angels. When all these fantasies don't come to pass as anticipated, the result is frustration and tension within the marriage relationship due to the un-met goals.

In America, where a significant number of marriages end in dissolution, some have argued to do away with marriage altogether, just like we may do away with any further invest-ments in business ventures which end up in insolvency and dissolution. Some of those who have burnt their fingers in the aftermath of divorce, with lengthy and expensive judicial processes, advise aspiring entrants into the marriage crucible to avoid it like the plague. Women's civil rights movements in America and feminist advocates from the 1970s onward have accused the Word of God of being biased against wom-en and leveraging their male counterparts to subjugate and subordinate them in marriage.[2]

---

[2] Letty M. Russell, ed., *Feminist Interpretation of the Bible* (Philadelphia: The Westminster Press, 1985), 11-18.

Some men feel shortchanged by some of the legal amendments that safeguard women's rights against domestic abuse without due process. Charges raised against men include rape within a marriage, which for some, is overly incriminating and unjustified. There are also cases of unfavorable decisions against men regarding child custody rights and the division of family wealth. Some men argue that the legal system, enforcement, and social structures all work to favor women whenever there is a disagreement between couples. These are among the reasons men choose to go on a marriage strike and shun the prospect of ever getting married.

Pressure from the feminist movement for women's equality at workplaces soon extended to homes, and the family unit has never been the same. Most women, who could not find equality in the home or in the family setup, opted to walk away from the shackles of their marriages and sought freedom by living without husbands. Their perceptions of marriage became so negative that some saw it as an unjustifiable window that accorded husbands the right to commit repeated rapes on their wives. Resentment for marriage among feminist women was so huge that taking up their husbands' names after a wedding became unacceptable. The right to secure abortions without consulting their husbands came under serious challenge as it amounted to controlling women and preventing them from taking full charge of their lives.

The family unit has come under attack from all fronts. It has rarely known peace. Children born in these tempestuous homes become deviant and antisocial. They set society on fire. Yet, when they grow up into adults and have their own families, they read from the same scripts their parents were reading and become just like them—doing the exact same things, and the cycle goes on and on. Other areas of interest are gender roles, sexuality, finances, and parenting. We may not have the time and space to go into the depths of these issues in this primer, but hopefully, we can at least take a cursory peep at each.

There seems to be tremendous confusion and turmoil in and around the institution of marriage from the foregoing. Some marriages take off well with lots of gusto at the beginning, but as time goes by, they go flat and even stale. Without timely diagnostics and troubleshooting, spouses have found themselves outside of the love zone, posing as roommates, co-parents, or business partners. When a marital relationship deteriorates to that extent, the vital sap that keeps marriages together is depleted, and therefore, there is no marriage. Something must be wrong; otherwise, God would not initiate and flag off the act of matrimony and have the audacity to call it "a good thing" if the craziness highlighted above is what he meant for marriage. Where do spouses go wrong?

Chapter One:
DEFINING MARRIAGE

T he term marriage might sound familiar, but it means different things to different people. Different cultures and communities synthesize and affix various values and meanings to marriage. From a social standpoint, what constitutes a marriage, or a family, has elicited diverse responses based on community, culture, economics, worldview, and religion. For instance, in the West, a man and a woman may live together and even have children; but in the absence of a civil or a religious tying of the knot, the relationship remains that of boyfriend and girlfriend. But, in many African and Asian communities, such a union could be referred to as a marriage, with or without tying of the knot. In Africa, boyfriend and girlfriend relationships are informal and morally shunned. They are mainly a preserve of teens and adolescents and are looked at as being deviant and untoward most of the time.

However, from a biblical standpoint, marriage in both the Old and the New Testaments is depicted as being sacred. In the Old Testament, the term marriage is used as a metaphor to describe God's relationship with his people Israel. Jeremiah 3:14 says, "Return, faithless people,' declares the Lord, 'for I am your husband. I will choose you – one from a town and two from a clan – and bring you to Zion.'" In the New

Testament, it is used to symbolize the unity of the Church with Christ. In Ephesians 5:31, Paul is quoting Genesis 2:24, which says, "For this reason a man shall leave his father and mother and be joined to his wife, and the two shall become one flesh."

The Apostle points to the metaphor in verse 32, saying, "This is a great mystery, but I speak concerning Christ and the church."

Paul uses the word "mystery" in referring to this scripture because it carries a deeper meaning and symbolism in the sense that the union between a man and a woman in marriage mirrors the unity of the Church and Christ. The Bible is replete with typology through which God's revelation of his divine working is exemplified through things and events on earth. For instance, the shadow of Joseph, the beloved of his father, who was hated by his own people but saved them from starvation, mirrors Christ Jesus, who was also hated by his own people and was falsely accused and condemned but brings salvation to his people.

Perhaps, what stands out in all of the quotes where God talks of his relationship with his people Israel in the symbolism of marriage, is the alluded *permanency of the relationship*. In Hosea 2:19, he says, "And I will betroth you to me forever. I will betroth you to me in righteousness and in justice, in steadfast love and mercy." As we continue to unpack the mystery of this divine ordinance, let's remember the quintessential attribute of permanency that has kept coming out.

From a biblical standpoint, marriage and family have a lot of common ground under them. A thorough distinction and compartmentalization are necessary to understand when we could be wrong to say we are in a marriage relationship while we could hardly be in such a union at all. Similarly, people could be living in an entity that appears as a family, but when interrogating the very essence of their living, they don't pass the test to be called family.

Both marriage and family were constructs of God at Creation. He initiated, ordained, and flagged them off in the Garden of Eden: "And God said, 'It is not good for the man to be alone; I will make him an help meet for him'" (Genesis2:18 [KJV]). So, when Eve was created and united with Adam as his wife, they became family, so to say. The Bible continues to say, "Therefore shall a man leave his father and his mother, and shall cleave unto his wife: and they shall be one flesh" (Genesis 2:24 [KJV]). From a biblical viewpoint, their union is what can be called a "marriage" and the unit "family." Let us now critically look at the union of Adam and his wife, Eve, to see why it is accurate to refer to it as "marriage" and why it would be inaccurate to label some other unions as marriages or families because they would not pass the test to be referred to as such.

A distinctive aspect of marriage that should always be at the back of our minds, whenever and wherever we are re-ferring to it, is its *heterosexual nature. It is always a man and a woman who can form a marriage and change their statuses into husband and wife.* It is the only accepted biblical position. Remember, after God created Adam, he discovered he was lonely, and it was not "good." Hence, God went ahead and created animals and birds and handed them over to Adam as pets to provide him with companionship, but their company wasn't capable of taking away his loneliness because, among all those pets, none of them could give him *true* companionship (Genesis 2:18-20). Not until Eve comes on the scene does Adam's loneliness and solitude find a resolution. This can also serve as a red flag for those of us who, after being let down by our spouses, resort to getting company and companionship from our pets. Seeking companionship from all the wrong places, including pets, is all a mission in futility and the height of depravity. True and biblical companionship only comes from a human *heterosexual relationship* involving a man and a woman.

Furthermore, to elevate our pets and give them the dignity and honor that befits humans is a serious distortion in the hierarchy of the created order. The elevation I am talking about includes referring to pets by masculine or feminine pronouns such as he/she, him/her, or his/hers. Pets are not made in the image and likeness of God for them to get the honor and treatment reserved for human beings. It may sound mean and insensitive but, with due respect, I would like to appeal that we go back to the scriptures to find our way especially, Genesis 2:20 [NIV], which says, "So the man gave names to all the livestock, the birds in the sky and all the wild animals. But for Adam, no suitable helper was found." This clearly says that Adam could not find a suitable companion or help-meet among the animals and all the pets. As pointed out above, authentic companionship only comes from a fellow human and one of different sex.

Let us continue with Adam's complement of Eve upon God's presentation to him. He says, "This is now bone of my bones, and flesh of my flesh: she shall be called Woman, because she was taken out of Man" (Genesis 2:23 [KJV]). First, we can see how Adam identifies with his wife by referring to her as bone of his bones and flesh of his flesh. Notice the depth and force in his choice of words; they effectively relay the consuming obsession and love toward his better half. The power of their union's bond emanates from beyond the heart, transcending deeper into the soul and the spirit. This is authentic love, not fake or generic. It is the super glue that binds the husband to his wife in a true marriage relationship. Anything less binding than that is a false, phony, or pseudo-marriage.

The second attribute that comes to the fore in Adam and Eve's matrimony is the act of becoming *"one flesh."* The mystery of *"one flesh"* is the mainstay of an authentic marriage, yet many couples are completely in the dark as to what it connotes. Moreover, lots of unions that do masquerade as being marriages have never attained this quintessential threshold even though the "couples" could be living together in the same home with children born out of their relationship. Marriages that come short of attaining this threshold of being "one flesh" are never stable but in perpetual turmoil and meltdowns.

Let's use the prototype union in the analogy of human fertilization, which involves the fusion of the human egg and sperm in the ampulla of the fallopian tube, to explain the nature of the union between a husband and a wife in marriage. The fusion of the two reproductive cells, the ovum and the sperm, lead to the formation of *one cell* called the zygote, which initiates prenatal development. It is important to note that the zygote is neither an ovum nor a sperm but a fertilized egg. Likewise, when a man and a woman get married the biblical way, there should be a marked change in their psychological, cultural, spiritual, and social status, congruent with the seriousness of the life-transforming commitments and obligations that come with the divine ordinance of marriage. Of utmost importance, they must become *one flesh.*

Some spouses have entered their nuptials without the necessary change from their previous selves, and the results have been tragic. Marriage is so serious an undertaking that those who enter it must be awake to that fact. Those who tie the knot and continue with their former lovers behind the scenes have had to pay a high price in terms of dysfunctional marriages, separations, divorces, suicides, murder, etc.

For a marriage to operate at its optimum level and serve the noble purpose for which it was created, all functions must work according to God's design and original plan. Every word in his pithy inaugural statement contained in Genesis 2:24 is worth serious consideration to keep things from running haywire in a marriage. When he said, "therefore shall a man *leave* his father and his mother..." what does he exactly mean in this admonition? Of course, there is the superficial meaning of leaving the parents' homestead and starting their own, but there is a deeper meaning to it also. Breaking off from the dependence, security, and comfort of the parents could be an emotionally, spiritually, physically, and even socially draining event, but it must be undertaken anyway for a marital relationship to operate normally. This doesn't necessarily mean that you must sever all links with your parents but reposition your relationships so that the one between you and your spouse takes precedence over your parents'. The newlyweds' relationship with their parents should become secondary, so they have the time to focus all their attention on their marriage.

Quite often, interference from the bride and groom's immediate or extended families has been responsible for the failure to thrive, which has been experienced in some young marriage relationships. Those parents and siblings in the know keep their social distance to nurture the young relationship into maturity.

The newlyweds are also admonished to leave *all* past opposite-sex friendships and everything to do with single lifestyles. This ought to have taken place during the long period of dating or pre-marriage counseling. Pictures, presents, or gifts from past opposite-sex relationships, if possible, should be discarded to ensure the bride and the groom have undivided attention to themselves and, therefore, enjoy a strong relationship borne of one flesh.

Bear in mind whenever God has wanted to do a great thing that could serve as a milestone in the lives of his people, he gives the command to "leave." When he wanted to set aside Abraham to become the father of his holy nation, he called him out and commanded him to *leave* his country, his people, and his father's household (Genesis 12:1 [NIV]). Abraham was being ordained for a special mission. Leaving or to leave carries the connotation of separating. Throughout scripture, to leave/to separate have the sense of setting aside for a special purpose which is an act of ordaining. All ordained/separated/devoted things are done so to the Lord and are therefore holy, as they are exclusively used in their functions to serve God. When a man leaves his father and mother, and the woman does the same, it can be interpreted to mean that they are being set aside or separated to respond to a higher calling of serving as a divine motif symbolizing the unity of the Lord and the Church. To all extents and purposes, the husband and the wife are out on a holy or divine assignment. Marriage is essentially meant to be holy. It is for that reason that the author of Hebrews 13:4 says, "Marriage should be honored by all, and the marriage bed kept pure, for God will judge the adulterer and all the sexually immoral."

Just as the sperm and ovum's fusion is permanent and irreversible because the cells cleave to each other to form one cell—zygote, so the husband and wife are meant to cleave to one another for life. That is what is meant when he says, "Therefore shall a man leave his father and his mother, and shall *cleave* unto his wife: and they shall be *one flesh*" (Genesis 2:24 [KJV]). Cleaving gives an immediate connotation of *permanency* and is the reason a married couple should have an inseparable emotional and spiritual bond that cannot be weathered by anything except death. Lack of money, employment, housing, food, or even children should not break a marital union, nor should disability or sickness.

Flirting or dressing indecently in revealing attire undermines the principle of being one flesh with the other spouse. Sexual intercourse has been alluded to as being a way of getting to be one flesh with the other partner. The sexual intimacy involved is responsible for driving those involved to the level of being one flesh. Paul warned the church in Corinth against sexual immorality that had become synonymous with the thriving port city of Corinth, "Do you not know that your bodies are members of Christ himself? Shall I then take the members of Christ and unite them with a prostitute? Never! Do you not know that he who unites himself with a prostitute is one with her in body? For it is said, 'The two will become one flesh'" (1Corinthians 6:15-16 [NIV]).

Even though this scripture reaffirms that one way of becoming *"one flesh"* is by way of sexual intercourse, being one flesh is not limited to sex alone but also includes many other day-to-day activities like praying and worshipping together, sharing information about our bank accounts or our savings, paying our bills together, caring for each other, sharing whatever we have without an iota of selfishness, loving each other, and sacrificing personal comforts to please the other, empathizing with each other, affirming and validating each other, caring for our children together, sharing every single secret in our lives, and protecting each other even in the face of death (this role is mainly a function of the husband), etc.

Not forgetting that by being one flesh, the body of one spouse belongs to the other, Paul says, "Nevertheless, to avoid fornication, let every man have his own wife, and let every woman have her own husband. Let the husband render unto the wife due benevolence: and likewise also the wife unto the husband. The wife hath not power of her own body, but the husband: and likewise also the husband hath not power of his own body, but the wife" (1Corinthians 7: 2 -5 [KJV]). Paul continues to emphasize this cardinal principle of kingdom living in the next verse, saying, "Defraud ye not one the other, except it be with consent for a time, that ye may give yourselves to fasting and prayer; and come together again, that Satan tempt you not for your incontinency" (v5).

Therefore, from the foregoing, there should be no such thing as rape within a marriage though we have legislation for it, pursuant to agitation by feminist rights groups.

Marriage is not meant for trial or as a contract one can enter and leave at will. God the Creator, who made humans and initiated marriage, laid out his plan for a lifelong sacred bond. Adam didn't ask God for marriage because he didn't know about it, but the Creator knew and designed marriage in his own wisdom. He planned and designed it in a manner that could work best for both Adam and Eve and unto their utmost mutual satisfaction. When used right, marriage, like electricity, gives you a fabulous service, but it becomes a tragic and deadly explosion when misused. Millions upon millions of people have had their lives shattered, terminated, or ruined forever because of marriages gone awry as a result of not following God's design.

As a lifelong commitment, marriage should not be dissolved except in very special circumstances, as provided for in the scriptures. One such circumstance is when one of the spouses is guilty of sexual immorality and is not willing to repent and live a morally responsible and Christ-honoring life. Another instance when a Christian marriage may be dissolved is a case where one of the spouses may not be a believer, and he/she decides to permanently walk out of the marriage (1 Corinthians 7:15). We are working with the assumption that *there is no domestic abuse and violence in "one flesh" marriage relationships.*

It is important to remember that even in the case of sexual impropriety on the part of one spouse, if the other has not been hurt so deeply that they can't recover, then forgiveness can be exercised, and they can try once more to live morally upright and acceptable lives before the Lord. Again, this is dependent on the level of grace operating on the infringed spouse; otherwise, divorce or separation may be the only options in such a case.

However, due to the devastating results that follow the dissolution of a marriage, it is important to take time to pray to seek God's direction on the matter and try as much as possible not to utter words that may inflict permanent injuries to each other's emotions and feelings. It is prudent to seek professional marriage and Christian counselors before proceeding to dissolve a marriage. This is because the family unit is the critical element that determines the community's functionality as a subset of society. It follows that functional marriages give rise to functional families, which in turn create good communities or neighborhoods and vice versa.

It is noteworthy that the husband and wife must live in a harmonious relationship for the family to function optimally. Acrimonious and dysfunctional marriages finally end in divorce most of the time. On the other side, the dissolution of marriages renders families dysfunctional and incurs deep scars of psychological and emotional hurt. The impact of divorce on children is more pronounced and tantalizing than on adult victims. For this reason, the family, as an entity of society, must be guarded against disruption if we want to populate our communities with emotionally secure and stable people.

Moreover, the family and the church are like two faces of the same coin. A family is the basic unit of human organization in the created order. That is why if the family flounders, the church flounders too. In other words, dysfunctional families beget dysfunctional churches. Knowing that to be the case, Satan has since changed tack, and instead of attacking the church directly, he simply attacks the family to send the church into a fatal stupor. Otherwise, if the church comes under attack from Satan, it can easily overcome when and if the family units are intact and focused. But, when Satan attacks the family, the church gets a fatal blow and often never recovers unless it enrolls new members.

Jesus responded to the Pharisees' question by referring to God's initial plan at Creation, saying, "But from the beginning of the creation God made them male and female. For this cause shall a man leave his father and mother, and cleave to his wife; And they twain shall be one flesh: so then they are no more twain, but one flesh. What therefore God hath joined together, let not man put asunder" (Mark 10:6 – 9 [KJV]).

As we analyze Genesis 2:24, let's examine in greater detail what it means "to *leave* one's father and one's mother ...."

Leaving is more than the physical relocation from one address or community to another. It is an emotive action that involves the mind, heart, body, and soul. If the body leaves, but the mind and soul remain in the family of origin, the marriage bond will be very unstable. Therefore, stability in marriage depends on how completely the spouses were able to leave their families of origin. A good number of marriages have experienced bonding difficulties for up to ten years or more after tying the knot, the reason being the incomplete leaving from their father's families.

I recently talked with a gentleman in Nairobi, Kenya, who is in his early 50s. He confided that he quit his marriage with his children's mother because she was completely unable to leave her parents' home even though they had been married for twenty years. They lived together in their matrimonial home, but her heart, mind, and soul were still back in her birthplace. The husband complained that the wife proved to be disloyal to her matrimonial home. She ran down the family business a couple of times by secretly sending proceeds from the family business to her mother and her siblings. She never stood with her husband, even once, to help the family prosper. All along, she behaved like a stranger or a hireling in her own matrimonial home. That is typical of a failed *leaving.*

Genesis 19 records the story of the destruction of the twin cities of Sodom and Gomorrah because of their extreme perversion. The angels who came to rescue Lot and his family told them to leave, run for their lives, and not look back. However, Lot's wife could not resist the urge and did look back, perhaps when she remembered the drinking orgies she had left behind. The Bible says she immediately turned into a lifeless pillar of salt.

If we decide to *leave,* looking back should be the last thing we do because it is tantamount to dismissing ourselves as unfit for the calling placed on us as spouses. Mrs. Lot was trying to leave with only her body, but her mind, heart, and soul were left behind in Sodom. She disqualified herself by looking back, and God immediately changed her into a useless monument of salt archived for the purposes of telling the present generation and those to come about the danger of not keeping God's vows. They vowed not to look back, but she did look back with the attendant consequences.

Jerry, an only son to a wealthy large-scale wheat farmer in Kenya, had a colorful wedding ceremony with his sweetheart and proceeded for a three-week honeymoon in the island city of Mombasa. The two love birds agreed to have quality time together by shutting their attention to the world around them so they could concentrate on their bonding.

They powered down all their phones and electronic devices, and their whole world was just between them. However, one week into the vacation, Jerry excused himself and made a quick phone call to his mom to find out how she was doing. At the end of the honeymoon, they returned to their apartment adjacent to Jerry's parents' house.

Just a few weeks into the marriage, Jerry's sweetheart started whining that she felt unloved and lonely because Jerry spent most of his time with his mom and only came to bed late in the night. They talked it over, but Jerry couldn't break loose, and being an only child, his mom adored him immensely. You may not be surprised that Jerry's marriage was stormy most of the time, and they finally divorced. A divided heart cannot sustain a healthy marriage relationship.

Wise parents should learn to give their offspring the support and space they need to nurture their young marriages.

Chapter Two:
SUBMISSION AND LOVE

BACKGROUND:

*T*he most controversial subject on marriage right now could be on the submission of a wife to her husband's authority in alignment with 1 Peter 3:1-8. Most pastors would hesitate to preach on this subject for fear of the reprisals it is likely to elicit from certain women's quarters, which may split the church. Even though God, as the author of the institution of marriage, has given instructions on the conduct and preservation of marriage relationships, the Enemy has exploited the little ambiguity on the matter of wives submitting to their husbands to incite and set couples to work at cross purposes, contrary to God's design for the sacred union.

Some educated and privileged women have successfully carried out powerful campaigns. Starting in the United States and eventually reaching the whole world with a clarion call for every woman to challenge the status quo that undergirds a patriarchal system that favors men and sets women as lesser beings. They argue that the male-dominated society relegates women to playing the underdog, and they are subjugated and denied equal treatment with men. The prospect of husbands exercising authority over their wives is seen as an escalation of the patriarchal oppression that denies women their right to make decisions concerning their own lives, destinies, children, dressing, education, and just about everything concerning women folk. The rivalry between husbands and wives has been so great that the first and second waves of the feminist movements, which champion women's rights, detest marriages and see them as oppressive prisons from which women need to be emancipated. The Evangelical feminists, who are in the vanguard of promoting gender equality and opposed to male headship, have gone many steps forward, advancing an argument that at Creation, Adam was sexually undifferentiated and that his humanity was what was important for his incarnation, not his maleness.[3]

This supremacy feud has inflicted irreparable injuries in the hearts of those women who feel misused and abused by the male-dominated society. They argue that even the state laws that legalize marriages are being used against women's welfare by condemning them to marriages that serve as prisons to incarcerate them until their death. No wonder the strong advocates for the women's movement are against marriage between women and men, preferring to remain single or marry fellow women in lesbian relationships. The discontent among those with heavy feminist underpinnings is so great that they seem to be at war with not only society with its patriarchy and state laws that sanction marriage but with a gendered God who elects to be called "Father" instead of a gender-neutral term like "Parent." This fallout stretches back

[3] Stanley Grenz and Denise Muir Kjesbo, *Women in the Church: A Biblical Theology of Women in Ministry* (Downers: Inter Varsity, 1995), 207-209.

to the 19th century when a group of women led by Elizabeth Cady Stanton recognized that something had to be done to counteract the oppressive power of the Bible. This culminated in the publishing of the *Woman's Bible,* which corrected what they termed cultural biases that distorted women's freedom.[4] Gender-neutral Bibles such as New Revised Standard Version [NRSV], New Living Translation [NLT], and The New Living Translation [TNIV] remove thousands of male-oriented words, replacing them with gender-neutral ones. The muting of the masculinity of many passages of scripture has achieved the feminist goal of denying anything uniquely masculine.[5] The fighting seems endless, and the gap between the feminist proponents and the menfolk is ever-expanding. An idea that God inaugurated with the best of our interests and His has been twisted with unsavory results. Evangelical feminists, along the way, endorsed homosexuality in the Church, a Mother God, and a female Jesus, all in the name of rejecting male headship and submission.[6]

I recently talked with a lady who expressed extreme disappointment with her ex. She said that the man was so irresponsible and did very little to help the family move forward. He only loved his boat and could go fishing most of the time while she ran helter-skelter to provide for the family and pay the mortgage and other bills. Moreover, he was cheating on her. This lady said that she got so upset that she decided to

---

[4] Letty M. Russell. ed., *The Feminist Interpretation of the Bible,* 24-25.

[5] Wayne Grudem, *Evangelical Feminism: A New Path to Liberalism?* (Wheaton: Crossway, 2006), 223-224.

[6] Luc Christiaensen, "Domestic violence and poverty in Africa when the husband's stick is like butter," *World Bank Blogs,* January 18, 2016, https://blogs.worldbank.org/africacan/domestic-violence-and-poverty-in-africa-when-the-husbands-beating-stick-is-like-butter.

marry a dog, which she has found to be a far better companion than her ex! Yet another lady professor who had divorced told me that her ex could not think. He was just a zombie or a big baby, she got fed up with him, married a fellow woman instead, and life went on much better after that.

Of course, some men have misused their physical strengths and positions in their families as heads to abuse their wives physically, verbally, emotionally, and psychologically. In Africa, the violation of women's rights and domestic abuse are more pronounced, especially among the rural poor populations with lower literacy levels. In the process, some rural married women have come to believe that abuse and abasement are part of the marriage package that women must learn to bear[7]. Churches have advocated for change in the status quo, so women are treated with love, honor, and respect the way God meant it to be.

From the above trends, it is apparent there could be a serious disconnect or gross misunderstanding on how marriage ought to be initiated, maintained, and preserved. Marriage is the glue that holds a family unit together and is a critical component of society for which everything needs to be done to ensure it runs optimally. Otherwise, if marriages are made to malfunction, society will soon grind to a halt, with chaos erupting in every family. Humans, as social beings, operate at their best when they live in small colonies or family units. In these colonies, we get the emotional support we need to recharge and continue in the journey of life. That is what God was addressing during Creation when he said, "It

[7] Wayne Grudem, Evangelical Feminism: A New Path to Liberalism? (Wheaton: Crossway, 2006), 223-224.

is not good that the man should be alone; I will make him an help meet for him" (Genesis 2:18 [KJV]). Marriage provides several psychological benefits, such as enhanced feelings of meaning and purpose in life and an improved sense of self-worth.

A journal for health published by Harvard Medical School says compelling research suggests that married people enjoy better health than single people.[8] It further states that compared to single people, married people tend to live longer, have a lower chance of becoming stressed, are less likely to have advanced cancer at the time of diagnosis, and are more likely to survive cancer for a longer period of time. Married people are more likely to survive a major operation than single people.[9] *Therefore, benefits for married people are wide, including improved immune systems, higher chances of survival from heart attacks, and more rapid recovery in the event of heart surgery.*

Of course, those who have dysfunctional marriages, in other words, marriages operating outside of the Creator's provided operation manual, don't enjoy the above benefits because they are operating off-limits and are disobedient to God's command. They are living in rebellion. Put differently, from a theological perspective, those living in God-honoring marriages where couples operate in love as *one flesh* enjoy God's matrimonial blessing. From the raft of blessings or

[8] "Marriage and Men's Health," *Harvard Health Publishing*, July 2010, Updated June, 2019, https://www.health.harvard.edu/mens-health/marriage-and-mens-health.

[9] "Marriage and Men's Health," *Harvard Health Publishing*, 2019, https://www.health.harvard.edu/mens-health/marriage-and-mens-health.

benefits, if you will, which follow those who choose to get married, we can safely conclude that God is pro-marriage. His favor comes to those who marry, as they become mirrors of Christ and the Church. Even then, those who choose not to marry for religious convictions to dedicate their lives to serving God have their portion of God's blessings too.

While patriarchy has been used as a wedge to advance the arguments against marriage, we strongly believe such arguments are beside the point. If patriarchy, as promulgated by God, could be used in moderation and piety as a motif of the Godhead, the divine ordinance of marriage could have served the purpose it was meant to accomplish at Creation. Once we become alive to this fact, we should not continue playing into the gallery of the devil, who always tries to create confusion and despondency by twisting the truth and turning it into the exact antithesis of God's divine position. We need healing for hurting marriages, so the family unit, as the primeval building block of society, is restored to optimal functionality.

God always operates in a family within the Holy Trinity. His tri-personal nature comprising God the Father, the Son, and the Holy Spirit is a family of co-equals with designated roles. Marriage is essentially, therefore, a replica of God's very essence as put on display in the Trinity. At its best, marriage should be the embodiment of harmony, mutual love, sacrificial giving, selflessness, and joy.

REDEFINING SUBMISSION:

What, then, is the cause of the turmoil witnessed in many marriage relationships across the globe? Matrimonial relationships turn toxic and unsavory once they are worked out in ways that are inconsistent with God's original design. For instance, when God directs that wives must be submissive to their husbands, he means just that, and there is no way we can bypass this command. Similarly, when he commands husbands to love their wives just like they love themselves, he means exactly that; anything else backfires. Carrying out these directions has been a tall order for most people because they lack in-depth knowledge of what they entail. It, therefore, follows that those who take time to read scripture and seek God's revelation and direction on how to do marriage will have more meaningful marital relationships than those who simply jump onto the bandwagon howling, "come we stay."

From the above disclosures, let's try to go to the core of the million-dollar question about what God means by exhorting wives to be submissive to their husbands, as captured in Ephesians 5:22 "Wives submit yourselves unto your own husbands, as unto the Lord," or in Colossians 3:18, which says, "Wives, submit yourselves unto your own husbands, as it is fit to the Lord." Because of the complexity involved in unpacking this theological phenomenon, it may help to define the bits and pieces that comprise the whole. First off, submission does not mean subjugation. Next, submission exudes the godly character in the doer. Lastly, submission ensures orderliness which is a hallmark of the Godhead. For our God is a God of order (1 Corinthians 14:33).

Submission is an expression of intimacy extended by a wife to a loving husband. It is an act of unconditional self-giving that oozes trust and surrender. Elisabeth Elliot, contributing writer to *Recovering Biblical Manhood and Womanhood*, sets the bar for an ideal wife very high, saying that the bride surrenders her independence, her name, her destiny, her will, and herself to the bridegroom in marriage and in their marriage chamber she surrenders her body and her priceless virginity[10]. Elisabeth calls this true femininity. This is in alignment with what the Apostle Peter says when exhorting wives to be submissive to their husbands as that adds to their beauty, which is their inner self, comprising of a gentle and quiet spirit, which is of great worth before God (paraphrased 1 Peter 3:3-4). Peter reminded the ladies that their beauty does not come from elaborate adornment and fancy hairstyles but from the inner person, steeped in submission, if I may add.

When a wife submits to her husband, the God-image that is inside of her powerfully comes out and radiates her environment. Those are the godly or virtuous women King Lemuel is talking about. He says, "Who can find a virtuous woman? for her price is far above rubies. The heart of her husband doth safely trust in her, so that he shall have no need of spoil. She will do him good and not evil all the days of her life" (Proverbs 31:10-12 [KJV]).

See how this gentle and quiet spirit manifested itself in the response Mary, the mother of Jesus, gave to the angel Gabriel upon receipt of the Good News, "Behold the handmaid of

---

[10] John Piper and Wayne Grudem, ed., *Recovering Biblical Manhood and Womanhood: A Response to Evangelical Feminism* (Wheaton: Crossway, 2012), 398.

the Lord; be it unto me according to thy word" (Luke 1:38 [KJV]). Those beautiful words are the epitome of trust, surrender, self-giving, and loyalty. Submission, therefore, accentuates the charming, beautiful, and captivating feminine essence found in a wife.

Submission could be said to be the glue that binds a husband and a wife into lifelong soulmates. Nothing endears a wife to her husband more than an act of submission. No husband would like to waste a second away from his submissive wife. A doting husband cannot hesitate to lose even his own life to secure his submissive wife.

I once heard a story about a ship that broke down on the high seas, forcing all the passengers to scamper for safety with lifebuoys while others just dived into the water as the ship started sinking. There were only a handful of lifejackets, so only a few lucky passengers got some. One gentleman was swimming around the sinking ship in his jacket to locate the whereabouts of his wife. As he swam around, he heard a desperate voice choking with water saying, "Honey, I'm sinking; I didn't get a lifebuoy!" The gentleman, who was her husband, frantically tried to look for an extra jacket around the ship but couldn't find any. Meanwhile, the wife was crying and choking on water, as she was apparently not a good swimmer. Her husband couldn't stand the spectacle anymore; he quickly swam to where she was, removed his life jacket, and handed it over to her, saying, "Darling, I love you. Put on the jacket and wait for help. As for me, in case I don't make it, "farewell and bye, darling." Unfortunately, before the rescue team arrived to evacuate the passengers, the man succumbed to his death by drowning. I can't imagine a man who can hesitate to put his life on the line and even lose it because of a submissive wife.

Most marriage relationships lack the glow because they have not been electrified by submission. Submission is the hallmark of Christian living. Try it and see the difference; you won't regret it. Whereas submission ushers in the anointing that keeps a relationship alive, doing it the reverse way won't get the spark at all. Anytime we contradict the position given by God, we come under a curse, and things don't work out the right way. We get God's blessing, even on our children, only when we are compliant and at peace with his commands. Remember, Lucifer's main tactic is to work at cross purposes with any position taken by God. Satan is the exact opposite of God. God brings life, peace, joy, and blessing, while Satan brings death, war, sadness, and curses.

I once went to buy a used car from a neighbor of mine in Kenya, who was a top company executive. She wanted to sell the older car so she could create space in her garage for her new car, which she had just bought. The lady was the sole breadwinner for the family as her husband had lost a well-paying job and resorted to heavy drinking. The community held the lady in high esteem but saw her husband as being irresponsible and untoward. The lady had even taken a loan and started a big business for him, but he ran it down because of his drinking habits. She often had to pick him up from his drinking dens, drunk like a sponge, and get him back home.

When I went for the car, I knew it belonged to the lady as she had bought it a few years back. However, when I expressed my desire to buy the car, she said they were selling it, but she could not fix the price as that could only be done by her husband, who was unfortunately drunk at that moment. She advised me to watch on him and come when he was sober, so we could make a deal. It did not occur to me that an irresponsible husband, whom I had dismissed as a wretch, could be accorded such great respect and honor by the hard-working wife. I marveled at the lady's inexhaustible patience and love for a person I could call a careless husband. Even then, I came the following day when he was sober, and he told me he had been briefed. He then requested to know my offer, which I did, and before long, we settled for the selling price. He took the car documents from the drawer and beckoned his wife to come and sign the transfer documents. She dutifully came smiling and thanked us for making the deal.

I did not understand the significance of a wife's submission to her husband as much back then, but years later, I learned that God's blessing operates in wifely submission. Apart from this family being successful in most of what they did, their six children became role models in our community. They all respected and loved their father and assisted him in moderating his drinking. The man finally quit drinking and embarked on yet another huge family business enterprise, this time with lots of success.

"Every wise woman buildeth her house: but the foolish plucketh it down with her hands (Proverbs 14:1 [KJV]). I have witnessed homes where submission and headship in marriage have been switched, but what becomes of those families, to say the least, is pathetic. Anytime we work at cross purposes with the Living God, the outcome is never good but always nasty; because then we are operating under a curse. Children who are born into such homes will often have deep emotional problems and become poor spouses who cannot keep marriages. Children from broken homes perform poorly at school, and their graduation odds are minimal.

A good number of women, especially those with a background in feminist and women's rights crusaders, struggle with the issue of wifely submission. Those with a negative perception of submission take it to be the same as inferiority, which is not the case. Wives are never inferior to their husbands but operate as co-equals with gendered roles. When Jesus submits to the Father, he is not inferior to him but a co-equal. It should be remembered that submission involves voluntary yielding to the other and is ingrained in humility, which is the backbone of a godly and Christian character. We serve a God of order and not chaos or rivalry. To the extent that husband and wife are meant to have a lifelong relationship, God had to give express instructions to ensure couples don't run into self-disruptive and destructive tendencies of rivalry and unhealthy competition, which set families in turmoil.

It is very important for all who care to honor God's word to know that the submission of wives to their husbands that Paul is rooting for in Ephesians 5 is not something that he created himself, but it was God's command right from creation. When God created Adam and Eve, he had in mind a relationship that would mirror the relationship between Christ and the Church. The Church was not there back then (even though we know Christ was there, as part of the Trinity), but came to be revealed in the New Testament during the life and ministry of Jesus Christ. This is what Paul means by referring to marriage as being a mystery, which was, from the very beginning, a shadow of Christ and the Church (Ephesians 5:32). In *Husbands and Wives as Analogues of Christ and the Church,* George W. Knight III says, "Paul saw that when God designed the original marriage, He already had Christ and the church in mind... If this is so, then the order Paul is speaking of here (submission and love) is not accidental or temporary or culturally determined: it is part of the *essence of marriage*, part of God's original plan for a perfect, sinless, harmonious marriage."[11]

In conclusion, it should be noted that the issue of wifely, voluntary, and loving submission should be seen in the light of God's eternal purpose as a parable of the relationship between the Church (Wife) and the headship of the husband (Christ). Interpreting submission outside of these theological axes is unbiblical and outside God's original purpose. Therefore, it is grossly inaccurate to dismiss submission as a construct of a given culture or a leave-or-take proposition within a marital relationship. Submission is a core absolute that we must strive to attain to enjoy covenant blessing through a thriving and God-honoring relationship.

---

[11] John Piper and Wayne Grudem eds., *Recovering Biblical Manhood and Womanhood,* 176.

Chapter Three:
HUSBAND AND HEADSHIP

*T*he husbands' headship over their wives is one aspect of marriage that is most misunderstood, contested, and abused. To prepare the ground for argumentation on this emotive topic, let's qualify a few statements here. Headship or leadership is a mandatory requirement if two or more people are going to live together in peace and harmony. Humans, as social beings, bring out the best in them when they live and operate in well-organized groups with leadership structures clearly defined. Lack of leadership breeds chaos and anarchy.

When I was a teenager, I used to help my late mom split firewood, which we used for fuel to cook food in our home. We had lots of huge tree stumps on our farm, but I hewed most of them and gave my mom the firewood she needed to cook our meals. I learned quite early that to hew a stump with an ax, you need to start from the peripherals by removing small chips off the main stump. If someone started in the middle, intending to split the stump in the middle into two halves, that would turn out to be an arduous and time-consuming task. Let us, therefore, hew off smaller chips from the main stump of husband headship by referencing scripture.

When an argument arose among the disciples as to who among them was the greatest, this was a legitimate concern because they knew Jesus was about to go to the Father. There was, therefore, an urgent need to organize their group accordingly into clearly defined leadership structures. This could ensure that when the Lord had to leave, there would be no leadership vacuum which could have rendered the group dysfunctional. Jesus' response and subsequent illustration of what leadership entails could be a good starting point for understanding the doctrine of headship. "Jesus said to them, 'The kings of the Gentiles lord it over them; and those who exercise authority over them call themselves benefactors. But you are not to be like that. *Instead, the greatest among you shall be like the youngest, and one who rules like the one who serves*'" (Luke 22:25-26 [NIV]).

The guidelines the Lord gave to the disciples concerning Christian headship/leadership are critical for our understanding of husband headship over the wife. A husband does not need to lord it over his wife, nor does he need to be bossy. The husband should instead be the one who serves his wife. Headship is therefore anchored on serving and NOT to be served. Jesus says of his ministry, "…and whoever wants to be first must be slave to all. For even the Son of Man did not come to be served, but to serve, and to give his life as a ransom for many" (Mark 10:44-45 [NIV]).

Biblical headship, therefore, is one that eggs on husbands to serve and help their wives because of love as *"flesh of my flesh."* A loving husband, who helps in household chores, cooking, cleaning, etc., exemplifies what Jesus meant by leading through serving. *Servant leadership is sacrificial because it involves voluntarily giving up your own comfort for the sake of your spouse.* In servant leadership, we consider the next person as being better than us. Servant leadership is selfless; it is longsuffering, empathetic, God-honoring, and a trademark of the covenant relationship. John Piper says biblical headship for the husband is the divine calling to take primary responsibility for Christlike, servant leadership, protection, and provision in the home.[12] Husband headship can be summarized as comprising: *to serve, to protect, and to provide.*

Headship requires the husband to play out his priestly role as the spiritual leader of his family. When God came to check on what was going on with the primitive family at the Garden, he asked Adam to explain what had happened. God, being all-knowing, had, of course, known what had happened but wanted to get it from Adam because he was the one responsible for the family's spiritual upkeep (Genesis 3:9-12). As head, the husband leads the family in devotions to nourish and ground those of his household on sound doctrine and cause them to experience Christian formation. God's intention of electing the husband to be head was to have someone responsible for spiritual nurture in every family and, therefore, when the spiritual wellbeing of a family is wanting, fingers should be pointed at the husbands and fathers as having failed in their primeval responsibility. This means when the wife or the children live prayerless lives, the buck rests with the husband/father to the extent that spiritual upkeep for the family falls in his docket.

[12] John Piper, *What is the Difference: Manhood and Womanhood Defined According to the Bible* (Wheaton: Crossway), 66.

While there is no denying that some women/wives could be better leaders than men/husbands, God, in his divine wisdom, unequivocally ordained husbands to provide leadership at the family level. In the Old Testament, husbands also took the role of priests at the family level. Job used to offer sacrifices on behalf of his family. The scripture says, "And it was so, when the days of their feasting were gone about, that Job sent and sanctified them, and rose up early in the morning, and offered burnt offerings according to the number of them all: for Job said, it may be that my sons have sinned, and cursed God in their hearts. Thus did Job continually" (Job1:5 [KJV]). Husbands were, therefore, spiritual leaders, and there was no reversing of that role. To circumvent this command cannot bring the intended results which God had in mind when He inaugurated the ordinance of marriage.

Whenever I lead my family in bible study sessions, fasting, or intercession, it feels good and becomes a booster of self-esteem. Fellowshipping together as a family brings harmony, joy, and familial love and inculcates a feeling that we are a people with a mission. Our children join gangs and engage in all manner of antisocial activities when we fail to execute our mandate. Marital infidelity has a much lower chance of happening in couples who pray together and are conscious of their identity as a people called out into covenant faithfulness and as a people with a missionary intent. One thing we must know is that the children won't take family devotions seriously if the fathers don't attach significance to them. If, for instance, during the time allotted for bible study, singing, or prayer, the father gets engrossed in watching a sensational super bowl match between local champions, this will drive a wrong message to the children that the devotions are not all that important, after all. So, we must make sure that our family spiritual commitments take precedence over all else.

The family altar is a safe enclave where the children and everybody else in the family can hone their skills for prayer, testimony, memorizing verses, speaking, and preaching. Children get to be known by the type of family altars they were brought up in. If you are going to find children with the virtues of honesty, charity, chastity, temperance, kindness, humility, etc., more than likely, much of that must have been inculcated and invigorated at their families of origin. During the early years, when character is formed in children, that is the right time for the father, with the assistance of the mother, to imbibe those ideas into the lives of the precious young angels God has placed in our hands for Christian nurturance and upbringing.

If you see greedy young people, then you know that, at their family altar, they were not trained on generosity, benevolence, or sacrifice. Similarly, if you find children who are proud or envious, then you can speculate that they were never trained on modesty, satisfaction, or compassion. The values and norms held dear to a family will be passed on to the children, and that has a bearing on their later years. For this reason, uninvolved parenting, where parents don't really mind what goes on in the lives of their children, is un-biblical and not from God. In families where headship is in alignment with the word of God, great people who overcome the world will emerge, but in those families with spiritually deficient and uninvolved headships, you will find children and even parents struggling with habit-forming drugs and other forms of deviance.

As head, it's the *husband's responsibility to provide for the family and move the family out of the yoke of poverty.* Headship involves prudent use of the scarce resources available to the family by checking on unnecessary purchases and spending, so some savings are set aside for the rainy season. Squandering family incomes and engaging in wild spending sprees will open the family to a weak financial footing and suffering. A family with no savings or property ownership suffers a great deal of insecurity, uncertainty, and, to some extent, low self-esteem.

More importantly, *a husband as head owes his wife and children their physical and emotional security.* Scripture shows through the book of Proverbs that a good man leaves an inheritance for his children's children (Proverbs 13:22). A word of caution: Even though it is a good thing for parents to leave behind an inheritance for their children, they are under no obligation to save up everything for their children's inheritance while they themselves live in squalor and neglect. However, leaving an inheritance for children is a gesture of appreciating the children even as God the Father appreciated Israel and gave it the Land of Canaan for an inheritance (Psalms 105:11).

The husband, as the *head, has the responsibility of forging an elaborate working relationship between his family and their neighbors.* As members of the covenant-believing family, we are missional and outgoing, reaching out to our neighbors with love and the intention of winning them for Christ. Like salt to the world, we are meant to permeate our neighborhoods and create a presence for the glory of God. Effective headship requires that our families don't become pariahs but integral components of the communities where we live. Building social bridges with neighbors is contingent on the good reports and testimonies that follow our families. For this reason, the head of household has to ensure that members of his family enjoy a good reputation among their neighbors.

Chapter Four:
MARRIAGE AND CHILDREN

*A*s always, to understand God's intentions in commanding
Adam and Eve to be fruitful and to multiply, we must carefully retrace them from his creation order and divine character
(some have argued he never commanded but advised them).
Whatever he called into being and ordained at Creation has
an overarching eternal purpose of revealing his identity to
us. Have a look; scripture says, "Then God blessed them,
and God said to them, 'Be fruitful and multiply; fill the earth
and subdue it; have dominion over the fish of the sea, over
the birds of the air, and over every living thing that moves
on the earth'" (Genesis 1:28 [NKJV]). Of course, this is a
command. We must understand God as one who commands
or a dictator if we wish. He is absolute and perfect. In him,
there is no grain of falsity; He is the Alpha and Omega and
does not advise but commands.

When God blesses Adam and Eve and commands them to be
fruitful and multiply, it becomes clear that children are the
result of God's blessing. Children, therefore, are not a curse
but a blessing. The Psalmist says, "Children are a heritage
from the Lord, offspring a reward from him. Like arrows
in the hands of a warrior are children born in one's youth.

Blessed is the man whose quiver is full of them. They will not be put to shame when they contend with their opponents in court (Psalms 127: 3-5 [NIV]). If children are a blessing from the Creator, is it right to terminate fetal life through abortion?

As God's image-bearers, children should be received with thanksgiving and appreciation in the societies where they live. After finishing a discourse on divorce, Jesus rebuked his disciples for hindering little children who were being brought to him for blessings. "Jesus said, 'Let the little children come to me, and do not hinder them, for the Kingdom of Heaven belongs to such as these'" (Matthew 19:14 [NIV]). Those who opt not to raise children but keep pets instead are not responding appropriately to God's command to multiply and populate the earth. Is it right to love our pets so much as to elevate them to a stature equivalent to that of children and other family members? Bearing children will not be a prerequisite for entering the kingdom of heaven, but we should guard against treating pets as babies or children because they are animals and birds. In contrast, children are human, born in the image and likeness of the Creator.

However, those who, for some reason, are not able to conceive or to bear children should not feel condemned or unloved by God. Similarly, as Paul says, those who may choose not to be married or marry to dedicate all their time to serving the Lord do so to the glory of God (paraphrased) [1 Corinthians 7:36-38]. Noteworthy, much as immeasurable value is attached to children, couples should resist the temptation of fixing all their attention and time on their children at the expense of their marriages. Marriage should be understood as having been made to happen before the first baby came into existence and therefore deserves even greater attention. Sounds selfish, eh? But it is the way it should be while not neglecting the wonderful opportunity to care for and nurture our precious children. When children are born into dysfunctional marriages, they develop many emotional and psychological problems that render them socially maladjusted individuals.

It has been said that inmates on death row and other capital offenses are mostly from homes with dysfunctional marriages.[13] Children born into broken homes with dysfunctional marriages have been found to be low achievers in school, more likely to drop out of school, have poor immunity towards diseases, are more likely to commit suicide, have a higher likelihood to divorce when they get married, and suffer from low self-esteem. For this reason, a stable and functional marriage is imperative for bringing up emotionally, socially, and cognitively stable individuals. In fact, children need a stable marriage environment more than parents do. It is advisable not to have any children if the home environment is toxic and unsupportive of their emotional and psychological wellbeing.

Young couples sometimes experience disagreements once they have their babies, as their arrival necessitates many adjustments and changes hitherto unknown in order to accommodate them. Some husbands are known to have complained

[13] Bosick, S.J., & Fomby, P. (2018) Family Instability in Childhood and Criminal Offending during the transition into Adulthood. American Behavioral Scientist, 62(11) 1483 – 1504. https://dol.

of having been neglected as the wives cast all their energy and attention onto their newborns. However, as the babies grow, the mothers slowly start attending to the fathers, and the situation quickly normalizes. It is, therefore, important to be cautious not to neglect marriages and to leave them unattended over a long period of time, as that may create deep injuries that may take a while to heal. Remember, when marriages are in turmoil, society is in turmoil.

Needless to say, very busy work schedules may drain marriages to death. Therefore, it is important when picking work schedules that you consider to what extent it may eat into your marriage and deny you the much-needed family time. If it is only work, work, work, with little or no time for intimate spousal fellowship, soon you may have lots of money but no marriage or family. Allow nothing to distract you from focusing on your marriages, including working overtime at places of business.

Once everything gets situated within a marriage, the next invaluable step is to discuss and come up with parenting styles that can guarantee healthy kids who are emotionally stable and socially well-adjusted. Without paying due attention to this all-important responsibility, you will discover later in life that your children are not the blessing that God intended them to be at Creation. The scripture says, "Train up a child in the way he should go: and when he is old, he will not depart from it" (Proverbs 22:6 [KJV]). I know of many parents who have gone to their early graves because of the stress and disappointment emanating from their poorly raised children. At the same time, I have also seen thousands of parents who have lived longer because of the joy and fulfillment they derive from their well-brought-up and nurtured children. If you are going to invest more time, love, and careful attention to your little ones, you will, more often than not, harvest a good yield for your labor and vice versa.

One thing I need to repeat for emphasis is the need to have children while we have the capacity to do so. I once had a rare opportunity to connect and talk with a lady celebrity who had participated in the Miss Universe beauty pageant. I have never seen anybody more beautiful. Towering at six feet two inches, her slender mien and lovely and flawless face could not escape anybody's admiration, even at her sixty-plus years of age. She was a company CEO and was born again. She was a woman of noble character, endowed with every good quality you could expect of the best of women. She, however, never got married or had any kids. As we shared, it became apparent to me that this beautiful and highly successful lady wasn't happy about her life. She surprised me when she jokingly referred to herself as being 'useless' when I asked about her family and children. She talked to me as if she had done a crime for which she was sorry and remorseful. She told me, "I wasted my time traveling all over the world and forgot to have children or even get married." I was shocked by her response and reaction because, in my opinion, she had all the money, the beauty, and every good thing you could imagine.

As we continued to talk, I came to discover that she deeply regretted her decision not to get married and have children. At that point, money, her good looks, a nice job, etc., didn't seem to matter to her anymore. She was shouldering a heavy burden from the guilt of not having been married and raising her own children early in her life. In desperation, she was seeking to revamp her attachment to her niece, whom she was treating as an adopted daughter, but the girl wasn't very keen on that relationship as she had her own mother.

As we contemplate not raising children, let us remember a time is coming when our jobs will not be there anymore, our health will have failed, the beaming beauty will have faded, and even our teeth will have all gone, opening us up to the use of dentures, which we shall be removing and keeping away from our mouths, as we go to sleep. *During such times later in life, children come in handy as the perfect shoulders we shall be leaning on in our frailty.*

One feature that cuts across the social spectrum is that many years back, most parents brought up their children within a strict discipline regimen, which was at times enforced with heavy corporal punishments. However, as time went by, things have changed in most cultures today but not necessarily for the better. There is a tendency for most parents who were brought up with strict discipline not to subject their children to what they went through because they didn't like it. In such cases, those parents adopt a hands-off, permissive sort of parenting style, which is responsible for the deviant and headstrong kids we witness in society. So, what is the perfect or most effective way of bringing up kids who won't disappoint the community we live in and us?

Chapter Five:
PARENTING APPROACHES

I t has been said that parenting practices influence children's understanding of God. For a vast majority of children, the most influential context in their lives is the home. This is how the home environment is critical to a child's upbringing and character. Children's relationships with their earthly parents profoundly shape their understanding of God (Shaw W.H. Perry 2016). Quality Christian parenting will strive to reflect the character of God as a key element in nurturing the child's emerging relationship with God.[14]

Developmental psychologists have carried out many experiments to determine the best parenting styles, and many observations have been made on each of the four styles, namely: *authoritarian, authoritative, permissive, and uninvolved styles.*

Authoritarian parenting – A parent does not care about nurturing and tends to control the children with strict codes and instructions on what ought to be done and how. The absolute set of standards given by an authoritarian parent is not

[14] Perry W. H. Shaw, "Parenting that Reflects the Character of God," *Christian Education Journal: Research on Education Ministry* Series 3. Vol 13, No 1 (May, 2016): 43-58, (ATLA).

negotiable. Obedience is demanded from the children without questions.[15] Children have little room to express their own opinions or engage their brains creatively to come up with alternative ways of carrying out a task. If they ask why they are doing something the way they are doing it, the answer from the parent will typically be: "because I said so." Failure to carry out instructions and meet the standards set out leads to severe consequences that may involve tongue-lashing, strong disapproval, withdrawal of parental love, and even spanking. Authoritarian parenting does not involve persuasion, nurturance, or friendly interactions with the children.

Consequently, children brought up the authoritarian way are likely to do well in school because they fear the wrath of their parents if they fail to do well. They may be obedient and respectful, but they suffer from low self-esteem and other personality disorders. Children brought up by authoritarian parenting become socially incompetent and timid. They are more likely to suffer from depression. They become poor decision-makers because they were not given a chance to exercise their discretion or engage their minds creatively to solve problems. In the absence of direction from someone else, a child brought up by an authoritarian parent is unlikely to come up with a good solution to help get out of an imminent problem. They may be manipulative and given to lying—because, from their upbringing, lying was a survival technique.

[15] Ellen Greenberger and Wendy Goldberg, "Work, Parenting, and the Socialization of Children," *Developmental Psychology* 25, 1 (1989): 22-35, (ATLA).

Uninvolved parenting – the parents have little emotional involvement with their children and don't bother to know what goes on in the lives of their kids. They may provide for basic needs like food, clothing, and shelter but may not go to the extent of finding out what time they came home from a party or went out for a movie downtown. The degree of noninvolvement may vary from a little bit of concern to dismissive, indifferent, or outright rejection in terms of having any emotional engagement with the kids—reasons for such type of parenting range from drug abuse, busy work schedules, or marital disagreements.

Parents engaged in drug abuse may have little time of sobriety to interact with their children at a level where they connect lovingly in a child-parent relationship. Some of the parents feel that they lack the moral high ground to guide their children because they are so deep into drugs. Marital disagreements may also result in one or both parents keeping their hands off in matters involving the nurturance and guidance of their children. Yet, the one common reason for being uninvolved is the parents' engagement in two or more jobs. Parents, who work 12 to 16 hours a day, have no time to get to know what is going on in their children's lives. When children are not restrained or guided, they easily fall to peer pressure and engage in antisocial activities like joining gangs, smoking weed, shoplifting, etc.16

Children who are brought up through uninvolved parenting have low self-esteem, are low achievers academically, lack

[16] Kendra Cherry, "Uninvolved Parenting: Characteristics, Effects and Causes," Very Well Mind, July 17, 2019, https://www.verywellmind. com/what-is-uninvolved-parenting-2794958

self-control, are socially less competent, and are more likely to fall into anxiety and other emotional problems later in life.

Permissive parenting – also called *indulgent parenting,* is an approach where parents avoid making any demands on their children and are always responsive to their needs. They dislike disciplining their children as they shun confrontation. Permissive parents nurture and emotionally connect with their children. They are very loving and see even their grown-up kids as babies. Permissive parents treat their children as friends and can hardly correct them even when they are wrong. The children have lots of freedom and can virtually do anything without fear of getting a tongue-lashing from their parents. It is like the children guide themselves by engaging in self-regulation. The parents have little or no set standards of behavior and emphasize the children's freedom instead of responsibility. The parents are inconsistent in enforcing any rules that there may be and often use rewards or bribes like toys or gifts to have the children behave well. They bargain with their children and seek their opinion on any important decision.[17]

Research has shown that parenting styles have a big impact on children's behavior and personality, which they carry over into their adult lives. Because permissive parenting is characterized by a lack of rules and demands to be made, children who are brought up this way have a hard time regulating themselves in self-discipline. They do very poorly when it comes to observing rules and are likely to be unruly

[17] Diana Baumrind, "Effects of Authoritative Parental Control on Child Behavior," *Child Development,* (December 1966): 887-907, http://persweb.wabash.edu/facstaff/hortonr/articles%20for%20class/baumrind.pdf

in school. They are low achievers in school. Teens brought up under this approach have a higher chance of engaging in drug and substance abuse. Permissive parenting does not prepare children to be responsible members of society as they possess poor social skills, lack boundaries, and are demanding. These children make poor decisions as they have no previous experience in problem-solving and decision-making skills.

Because children brought up the permissive way lack boundaries and self-regulation, they struggle to manage their time and habits. They operate without limits and can watch TV, play computer games, or eat in excess. They become obese and are never at peace in their own skins—feeling ill at ease and insecure as though they are at war with everybody. This is definitely a style of parenting that every loving parent should shun.

Authoritative parenting – A child-centered approach in which parents lay a high threshold of standards and expectations which require children to strive to attain them while the parents provide them with needed support and encouragement. Authoritative parents encourage their children to give their opinions as they discuss the best ways of accomplishing expected tasks. The parents are nurturing and take time to listen to the children to boost their self-confidence. The child-parent relationship is warm and friendly. The parents talk and handle the children with respect to increase the children's self-esteem and personal worth.[18] The parents

---

[18] Diana Baumrind, "Effects of Authoritative Parental Control on Child Behavior," 887-907.

affirm and validate any good actions by the children and encourage them to seek the best solutions to solve conflicts facing them. The parents set limits, expectations, and consequences in the event of the children failing to achieve the set goals. Whenever the rules and expectations are not reached, the parents fairly administer discipline and make sure the children understand why they are punished. Authoritative parenting maintains and keeps consistency, so the children are not confused about what is right and what is wrong for them to do. Punishment may take the form of shutting off the TV, keeping the toys, taking away the tablet, withholding a gift, etc.

Children brought up with an authoritative parenting approach are the most socially competent. They have high self-esteem and are confident in what they do. They are emotionally stable and have the least personality disorders. The kids have self-control and a way of getting along with others. They are the least likely to have anxiety and depression issues later in life. Authoritative parenting helps children have a higher chance of academic attainment.

All the above approaches to parenting are material courtesy of the science called Developmental Psychology. We should be aware that we cannot afford to read and interpret scripture correctly without the help of other clusters of knowledge. Much as we tend to believe that science is against theology, it is time we realized that other branches of knowledge come in handy to enable us to interrogate the complex subject matter in the domain of theology and its allied corpus. I am not in any way contradicting my favorite philosopher,

Quintus Septimius Florens Tertullianus of Carthage, who, in his famous quip, asked, "What indeed has Athens to do with Jerusalem? What concord is there between the Academy and the Church? What between the heretics and Christians? Our instruction comes from the porch of Solomon who himself taught that the Lord should be sought in simplicity of heart."[19] The philosopher and Christian apologist was, of course, defending the Church against heresies, many of which were mined in Athens, the seat of the greatest philosophers and educators back then. Tertullian did not, however, dismiss all philosophy and science as being detractors of theology; otherwise, he himself was a philosopher.

In fact, philosophy can sharpen our capacity to reason and understand theology better. Even science may be aptly used as a tool to understand the complex subject of theology. However, while neither philosophy nor science can correct scripture, the latter can, on the other hand, be used to correct both philosophy and science. By giving scripture the authority and unequaled infallibility that it deserves, we can pick our cherries from all the other domains of knowledge so long as they don't run counter but help to understand the scriptures and their application. It is against this background that we picked the above parenting approaches, as elucidated by developmental psychologists.

Because marriage, children, and parenting are all ordinances and were promulgated by God at Creation, we shall treme ndously miss out on their very essence if we shall lose focus of God's original intention in institutionalizing them. Armed

[19] Vernard Eller, "On Prescription Against Heretics," in *The Reincarnation of Quintus Septimius Florens Tertullian*, 10,

with what we have so far learned about good parenting practices, let's now turn to the activities and practices that can help us to produce not only good children who will be invaluable assets to society but also children who will live God-honoring lives with a deep-rooted Christian formation, characteristic of the covenant family. To that end, we want to be intentional in picking biblical nuggets from here and there, which will help us to nurture and support our children to become what God wants them to be.

First off, love your children equally without showing any biases. Giving one child preferential treatment over the rest creates tension among the children. When others feel un-loved, they are likely to rise up against the one who is pre-sumed to be more favored or loved. Such tensions, many times, continue to manifest in their adult lives.

I have a life experience from my problematic childhood. As a little boy, the eldest in my father's family, I had a night-marish kind of upbringing with doses of countless lashes every day and, at times, twice a day. My parents were quite loving, but I was a small devil who stretched their patience to its limits. I sometimes wonder what was wrong with me that could have made me a tough nut to crack in those early years. I was argumentative and questioned why my parents were doing things the way they were doing them. They did not like such questions, and that got me in trouble all the time. I bullied my younger siblings because they kept laugh-ing at me whenever I was being punished. I could beat them up when our parents were away. But when my parents got back, I was reported and got countless whips. They again could taunt and laugh at me, and I could beat them once our parents were away, and the cycle went on and on. I was headstrong, and soon everybody came to know me as the imp that I was.

Some of my relatives condemned me and suggested that I be exiled from home because they thought the nurses might have swapped my mom's baby and given her a child that was not hers after her cesarean section in the hospital. Of course, I didn't resemble my mom in any way, having taken after my father. I was not good-looking either, compared to all my younger siblings, who all resembled my beautiful mom. To make matters worse, I had a very big head that made me the subject of ridicule in the whole village. Some never even used my name when calling me but simply called me "Big Head!" or "Cliff Head!" and so on.

I really had a rough time in my early formative years, and my self-esteem suffered irretrievably because of it. The only thing that saved me from further psychological and emotional breakdown was my performance at school. Right from preschool, I exhibited a rare genius and was moved to grade two during my first month in school and, at the end of the first semester, was promoted to grade three. I took fewer years to finish both elementary and high school. This gave a big boost to my low self-esteem and personal worth. I see the effects of my difficult background during my youth manifesting in my life to this today. I have also witnessed unhealthy tensions and rivalry with my siblings playing out over four decades later. My illiterate parents couldn't understand how to handle a problematic child; they simply felt overwhelmed. I truly sympathize and feel sorry for them. They unwittingly set my other siblings against me and warned them not to be like me. No wonder we have since remained rivals, which is debilitating to family unity. Parents should learn to handle their children as unique individuals with differences. Parents should not pit their kids against one another. Children should be taught to appreciate and love one another selflessly.

Do you remember the story of Rebecca? She was Isaac's wife, who bore twins but loved the younger of the twins, Jacob, who she led to steal the blessing of the elder twin, Esau, from their dying blind father (Genesis 27: 1- 40). It is important to note that the animosity that followed the fraudulent snatching of the eldest son's blessing by the younger continued forever. The descendants of Esau, the Edomites, moved and settled in present-day Jordan, and they have remained Israeli's arch enemies to this date. Joseph was hated by his brothers, who sold him to Egypt because he was their father's [Jacob's] favorite (Genesis 37: 3-5 [NIV]).

Once you have been equipped with effective parenting tools, the journey should not end there but continue to the nitty-gritty of day-to-day activities. These will serve in the grounding of the children on a solid and sound foundation for Christian living as you seek to gain an understanding of how to carry out the invaluable task of nurturing and growing our children in God-honoring principles in alignment with His Word.

Society has erupted with a generation of deviant and defiant youth who have wreaked enormous havoc on social tranquility and the pillars which foster harmonious living. Literally, every community is crying as the ground appears to have tilted, and the world appears to have been turned upside down. This is the magnitude of the problem the godless societies the world over seem to be experiencing. Murders, burglaries, carjackings, robberies, terrorist activities, and rapes have escalated in our global village. The main reason for this is that secularism has ravaged society unabated because fathers abdicated their primeval duty of leading their children to the Lord as he commands in scripture. Both in the Old and the New Testaments, God is emphatic on the husband's priestly role of steering his children in the way of the Lord.

The scripture admonishes fathers, "Train up a child in the way he should go: and when he is old, he will not depart from it" (Proverbs 22:6 [KJV]). This is a core duty that is mandatory for every dad if society is to produce responsible and God-fearing youth. To the extent that the family dutifully operates within the confines of the covenant promises in living out God-honoring lives, the blessing spoken of in Genesis during creation manifests to the glory of God. The million-dollar question is: how many of us, dads and husbands, play our roles effectively as priests serving at the family altar? Do we have structured activities in the daily family devotions to systematically introduce and entrench the children in salvation?

To be capable of executing the divine parental mandate upon their children, parents need to live cleansed lives and display an unswerving commitment to the ideals and imperatives of Christian living. You can only give that which you possess. You cannot give what you don't have. Parents can effectively train their children in the ways of the Lord if and only if they are born again and committed to the cause of the gospel and Christian witness. If, for example, a father does not lead his family in evening and morning devotions because he loves his sleep in the morning and watches his favorite football and basketball teams in the evening after work, the children will not take the word of God seriously. The children can best understand who God is by first observing their father, who is the Heavenly Father's closest motif. Uninvolved parenting, as said above, will only give us godless, deviant kids who will be a nightmare to society. But parents who lead through example and hold dear their testimony and Christian witness are likely to mentor, nurture, and bring up children that will be beacons of moral excellence and hope in the communities where they live.

Chapter Six:
MARRIAGE AND MONEY

O ne of the mightiest giants couples must defeat to make their relationships more mutually fulfilling, stronger, and God-honoring is the love of money. Agur made a petition to God in his prayers, saying, "Two things I ask of you, Lord; do not refuse me before I die: Keep falsehood and lies far from me; give me neither poverty nor riches, but give me only my daily bread. Otherwise, I may have too much and disown you and say, 'Who is the Lord?' Or I may become poor and steal, and so dishonor the name of my God" (Proverbs 30: 7-9 [NIV]). Money can puff up our heads and drain out any Holy Spirit that there might have been in us **if we let it be the center of our marital relationship.** When we centralize money at the heart of our marriages, it then takes the place of God and becomes an idol. Salvation can never be sustainable in hearts fraught with idolatry. Since I discovered the veracity of these soteriological truths, I have looked at money differently.

The Apostle Paul warned Timothy, saying, "For the love of money is a root of all kinds of evil, for which some have strayed from the faith in their greediness, and pierced themselves through with many sorrows. But you, O man of God, flee these things and pursue righteousness, godliness, faith, love, patience, gentleness" (1 Timothy 6: 10-11 [NKJV]). Paul knew that the people of Ephesus were money lovers to the extent that they did not want the gospel to be preached in Ephesus as that was going to interfere with their business of selling silver shrines of their fertility goddess Artemis (Acts 19:20-41). The love of money is a subtle way of practicing idolatry even to this day. Having money is not a sin, but loving it and putting it at the center of the heart and the soul constitutes idolatry which is the single worst sin that God detests.

Loving money means you can do anything so long as you are promised to be given payment. If you can give up your salvation in pursuit of money or prefer to work and make more money instead of going to church or weekly fellowships, then you are said to be a lover of money. If you have money, but it does not hold you captive nor interfere with your daily walk with the Lord, then it is not an idol of worship to you. Immoderate craving for money is an evil spirit that binds and holds people as slaves, not masters of money.

Remember, Paul does not condemn money itself in any way but the love of it. Yet, we understand that even the proclamation of the gospel witness will be slowed down without money. Jesus himself made use of money to settle bills, such as he did when he made payment for his taxes and the disciples' arrears, too, to the Roman authorities (Matthew 17:27). Therefore, Paul condemns the love of money and not money itself. Again, when he says that money is the root of all kinds of evil, he could be emphasizing or using hyperbole as an expression of the magnitude to which money may corrupt those who love it. Otherwise, we know of some evils done by humans that have nothing to do with the love of money— for instance, watching pornography or lust may not necessarily be due to the sinner's love of money.

As recorded in Luke 12: 15 [NIV], Jesus' stern warning is a priceless gem for Kingdom living. He warned, "Watch out! Be on your guard against all kinds of greed; life does not consist in an abundance of possessions." Even though the Lord did not make this pronouncement in the context of a marriage relationship, he nevertheless encompassed meltdowns and struggles witnessed among couples because of money. When the Lord sounded this exhortation, He must have seen past, present, and future marriage relationships which had gotten and will get dissolved at the altar of idolizing money. Being omniscient and all-knowing, he had the capacity to see even happenings into the future up to eternity. Therefore, the warning is a wake-up call for you and me lest our marriages disintegrate and we go separate ways, even with our beautiful children.

The highest and most loaded part of his statement is the last section which says, "life does not consist in the abundance of possessions." Possessions can surely not prevent you from dying when your time comes, nor can they enable you to inherit eternal life if you are not righteous before the Lord. Wealth and possessions may make us have false confidence or elevated egos about our capacities, but it is all deceptive fantasizing and the work of the flesh. Possessions may not give us the peace of mind, body, and soul the way *Shalom*

does. Our God is Jehovah Shalom (Judges 6:24). The He-
brew biblical greeting **Shalom** is used by the covenant-believing family to give a connotation of peace, harmony, good
health, prosperity, tranquility, welfare, protection, satisfaction, and joy. It can be used interchangeably to mean hello or
goodbye, with everything being anchored on Yahweh, who
alone provides the *Shalom*. Therefore, money cannot give
us the *shalom*, and to imagine or pretend that it could, is the
height of futility and human depravity.

In the context of marriage, money is the single second-
highest reason for divorce in North America today, second to
infidelity. Perhaps it is because most couples avoid discussing issues concerning money because they feel that if they
can trust one another for lifelong relationships, then money
will be just a small hurdle for them to go over. Some couples
draw cold feet when it comes to revealing their personal pro-
pensities and convictions to spend or save money, preferring
to discover each other's inclinations as time goes by. To the
extent that money has become a wedge that splits marriages
within no time, it is important that prospective spouses get
lots of counseling sessions on the use of money and how
it impacts marriage. They should also engage in sober and
open discussions on how they will want to use money in
their marriage.

The second reason why money may sometimes become an
emotive issue that can threaten a young marriage relationship's stability is that it means different things to different
people. There are those who see money as a means to an
end, while on the other hand, we have those who see it as

an end in itself. Also, there are those whose happiness is determined by the amount of money they have, yet still, some look at money as a source of security and a measure of self-worth or a status symbol in society. Because of the diverse worldviews, there is a dire need for sober conversations between couples on this matter unless both have a common ground based on solid Christian grounding, in which case they approach money from the biblical standpoint of being "one flesh."

The third reason is that how two different people view and use money has, to some extent, something to do with their families of origin. Quite often, when it comes to how to use money, children copy a lot from their parents once they become adults and active in the world of money. However, there are many instances where a partner may have come from a poor background, but once they get jobs and start getting their own money, they become great spendthrifts in a bid to compensate for the cash they may not have had earlier on in life. Yet, others from poor backgrounds may respond differently by becoming misers for fear that they might slip back into their former debilitating poverty. Either way, a middle ground must be mediated if the couple must live healthy balanced lives. Moderation is a household approach to doing stuff in a marriage relationship. Sharing each other's money stories is a great way of understanding your money-spending patterns with a view to striking some common ground.

I recently talked with a man who complained that he was contemplating divorcing his wife because she could not resist spending money to the last cent, so long as she knows it is there. He was saying that she buys impulsively, even those items she doesn't need. She likes outings and partying until all the money is gone, and then her craze subsides. He said that they had addressed the problem countless times, but it looked like spending was part of her DNA. I advised him to exercise patience with her and try out other methods of using money instead of the traditional and, of course, most commendable common pot method. Sometimes it becomes necessary not to disclose how much money you have in your bank account, especially when you know that your partner has an irresistible habit of impulse spending. Once the unhealthy habit is overcome and any wild spending is put in check, then you can slowly leverage back to the common pool method. Maybe you may need the Holy Spirit's direction on the matter so that you don't sin. Sometimes, spending or not spending has a lot to do with the mind's psychological frame and the entry behavior carried over from the family of origin.

Whereas couples come up with all manner of propositions on how to use their money, it can be argued that they are all good as long as they are able to win the approval of those concerned. The bottom line is to use money as a means to an end that involves harmony, satisfaction, and mutual fulfillment. Therefore, if the methods used don't create tension and disagreements, then those methods are commendable. However, some methods are more nurturing and inspire trust within the marriage relationship than others. Perhaps the greatest sin couples commit is to open personal accounts and set up passwords to ensure that the other partner does not get to know what goes on in the other's account. A couple is meant to operate as **"one flesh"** for a marital relationship to operate optimally. When your spouse has no idea of what comes into or out of your bank account, it creates mistrust and overthrows the essence of being "one flesh." **Trust** is the backbone of any functional relationship. The moment trust fizzles out, the marriage tumbles down like a domino.

On my part, I consider it unhealthy not to share with a spouse any personal passwords for access to any personal accounts. If we are operating within the divine mandate pronounced by God at Creation, the transformation of husband and wife into "one flesh" remains the overarching ordinance that all should strive to attain to enjoy the divine marital blessing that comes with obedience to our Maker's direction. When husband and wife are one, it goes without saying that nothing secret exists between them. My emails, text messages, and social media platforms are all open to my spouse because I hold nothing secret. Once we work out our relationships with openness, being fully accountable and submissive to each other, we assume a likeness of the Godhead. Can God hold back any secret from the Holy Spirit or the Son and vice versa? Openness and holding back no secrets are the best ways of inculcating mutual trust in a marriage relationship. Couples should determine the appropriate disclosure levels to move their relationships forward if that is what it will take to keep their marriages from sinking.

There might be some uneasiness in total self-disclosure, especially at the beginning when bonding is still taking place. Therefore, patience with each other comes in handy in the interim. Moreover, most marriage relationships start at their peaks during the honeymoon, but after that, the spark appears to be lost as couples adjust themselves to new realities in their new world. Sometimes, feelings of doubt and low morale creep in, and if the newlyweds had not been counseled and forewarned in advance, they may exterminate their budding relationship. Once the crisis after the honeymoon is gone past, the attachment steadily grows stronger and stronger, especially if there are no more headwinds.

Not forgetting that a bulk of the responsibility to provide for the family rests with the husband when families fare badly in terms of savings or investments, which could put the family on a weak financial footing; the buck will always rest with the husband. He is the head of the household. Husbands should, therefore, use their influence to ensure that families use their incomes wisely to ensure good savings for the winter. Unchecked spending, hedonism, and indulgent lifestyles undermine a family's financial grounding, which is a cause for countless squabbling and discontent in marriages.

Chapter Seven:
RESTORING THE FIRST LOVE

I have heard some speakers say that they have never disagreed or quarreled with their partners in all their married lives, but I have my fair share of qualms concerning their honesty. We could be born again and Spirit-filled, but we are still far from being perfect. Sometimes, we may fall into a foul mood and hurl careless words at our spouses in misplaced anger. The other may hit back in self-defense, and the home environment never remains the same. Human frailty is such that we are subject to failings, and it is the grace of God that keeps us from falling into deep sin. After some years of being together, marriage may feel boring and lackluster, especially when things seem not to be going well on multiple fronts. At times like those, we tend to wrongly think that the other partner could be the cause of the problems or misfortunes. In moments like those, you can start getting the feeling that you may not have been meant to be partners; it was just an unfortunate coincidence or accident. So, what should we do when the love that once lit our marriage is waning or not there anymore?

Many people enter into marriage with high expectations and assume it will supply solutions to most of their life's problems that they were unable to contend with previously. Some of the expectations even border on fantasy, but when reality sets in, disappointments and even regrets are not uncommon. You won't be surprised to find some who say that marriage is a bad thing that complicates life, rendering it a hoax and a waste of time. At the settlement of reality, you will hear all manner of accusations and counter-accusations for and against marriage. Yet, when God promulgated marriage and ordained it at the Garden, he said that it was good. It is more than likely there could be some disconnects or myths about marriage expectations that need to be put out of the way of your relationship to see things from their correct perspectives.

It is important to remember that marriage involves two people, each with different experiences from their families of origin and their cultural backgrounds. Two people with different worldviews and ways of doing things can only be yoked together when, among others, they are endowed with inexhaustible reserves of patience born of love. If you are not prepared with limitless reservoirs of patience, I advise you not to dare marry or get married. We need to be patient with each other at every step of the journey. Even the children, whom God places in our hands as custodians, test a great deal of our patience from the time they are born to the time they become responsible young adults. For, without patience, it is possible to get married in the morning, and by the time the sun sets, we shall be shopping for divorce attorneys to help in the dissolution of the relationship. That explains the centrality of the grace of patience in the cog's lubrication that turns the marriage relationship's wheels.

Bear in mind that if you don't love someone, it is almost impossible to be patient with them. Love can endure insults, injury, and provocation without burning with hate, resentment, and revenge. Love produces patience, enabling a partner not to develop the indignation to engage in verbal or physical abuse. Love produces perseverance, anchored on the hope that our partner will get over their weaknesses and become one who embraces peace and sensitivity to the other's hurt. Paul aptly captures this in his epistle to the Church in Corinth, saying, "Love is patient, love is kind. It does not envy, it does not boast, it is not proud. It does not dishonor others, it is not self-seeking, it is not easily angered, it keeps no record of wrongs. Love does not delight in evil but rejoices with the truth. It always protects, always trusts, always hopes, always perseveres. Love never fails..." (1 Corinthians 13:4-8 [NIV]).

If you hit an iron rod with a magnetic field hard with a hammer, it can lose its magnetism or be demagnetized. However, magnetism can be restored by simply rubbing it correctly against another magnet. Similarly, whenever the spark of love between a husband and wife seems to be dying out, steps to restore it can be retraced back to where the rain started beating the couple down. **Reconciliation** is a household activity for any group of persons who have chosen to be yoked together or to walk together. You can never be yoked together unless you are in agreement; otherwise, you will go opposite ways, and your journey will be impossible to accomplish. Therefore, it is imperative that disagreements and hurts resulting from careless words hurled at a partner can be gotten over by appropriately **tendering apologies.**

Whoever may be responsible for the careless word or actions that brought the hurt should, at the earliest, seek the audience of the aggrieved to **apologize and take full responsibility** for the misplaced anger or injurious statements made. The one who apologizes must **do so without trying to justify their actions or giving excuses for behaving the way they did.** Simply take full responsibility and tender your apology. Apologies, once done appropriately, in most cases, bring about instant healing and throw the relationship back on track. However, if an apology is made inappropriately, it appears insincere, and the injury continues to bleed.

Back in the day, when I became a pastor, we used to attend a month-long pastors' National Convention in Discipleship Training School in Kenya, where among others, we used to be taught how to preach and tend over the flock. There were, at any one time, at least five hundred ministers taking the in-service training. We used to sleep and eat there the entire time we attended the conference. The Director of the Bible School's wife oversaw catering with several cooks and caterers who made the challenging task of feeding over five hundred people, with three meals a day, a success. Occasionally, the last ones to be served could not find enough to eat, but on one particular day, almost one-quarter of the attendees could not find a plate of food to eat during lunch break. It forced the First Lady to take emergency measures to have more food prepared to serve those who had missed it. She was irked by some ministers' tendency to take double rations, especially when she served chicken. She complained aloud that the pastors should not eat as though they never eat in their own homes. Her complaint may have been legitimate, but when the pastors heard of it, they felt quite offended. Word quickly spread out that they were going to fast and boycott the First Lady's food for the days remaining before they could go back to their homes at the end of the convention.

When it was supper time that day, not a single pastor went to the dining hall for food. The cooks rang the buzzer several times, but no one turned up, and all the food went back. Both the Director and the First Lady were disturbed by the new development. Meanwhile, the pastors were embarking on their compulsory three-day fast, and they were not going to turn back since they felt slighted by the First Lady.

The following day started as usual, with the one-hour devotion at the chapel, where the faculty and the pastors were in attendance. When it came to the announcements, the First Lady made an unexpected and powerful apology for the statements she had made, which had irked the ministers to the extent of boycotting her food. With tears rolling down her cheeks, she started, "Dear pastors and faculty, I would like to report to you that I never slept a wink last night because of the silly statements I made against our pastors. I am so sorry and apologize from the depths of my heart and request that you forgive me. I won't make such careless and demeaning statements again. Even my husband has complained about how I sometimes make careless statements. If he were not a strong man of God, he wouldn't have had me for a wife. I beg that you forgive me and eat my food as you have done before."

As the First Lady was apologizing, some of the pastors went to their knees praying and apologizing to her as well. With tears flowing, the pastors said they were the ones who were wrong and not her. That day, there was a mighty movement of the Holy Spirit in the morning devotion like never before. **Reconciliation ushers God's presence into a relationship or group of persons.**

When we apologize and say we are sorry, we should take full responsibility for our actions without turning around corners to justify our actions. **Being defensive, in any small way, bursts the bubble and renders the apology emasculated and powerless. When an apology is given as it should be, the results are therapeutic, tantalizing, and instantaneous.**

One of the lowest and most unfortunate moments in a relationship is when **oral communication** is severed. Partners resort to writing text messages to each other even when they are both in the living room. We shouldn't allow ourselves to drop to that barbaric level. Let communication be ongoing no matter what, and if possible, orating face-to-face should always be maintained whenever possible. However much we could be offended, **marital courtesy requires that we answer each other's phone calls without fail** unless there is a legal requirement to the contrary. We are made in the image and likeness of God. That is the reason you may request a favor from a friend through a text message and get declined, but if you ask the same favor through a phone call or by physically meeting, chances of getting positive feedback are much higher because God's likeness shines in each of us and impacts us with a stronger punch. So, when we keep talking after we have disagreed, we are more likely to get over our differences within no time and vice versa.

Sleeping in different rooms or even beds should be discouraged as much as possible because it is one sure way the devil uses to drive a wedge between a couple and split their relationship in two. A couple is meant to be **"one flesh"** per the instructions of God at Creation. That command is the backbone of any functional marriage. The moment couples allow the Enemy to separate them, their marriages cease to evoke the sparks of joy and gratitude characteristic of thriving, God-honoring relationships.

If a relationship starts to turn sour during its first few years, and you find yourself in an unending blame game, do not be in a hurry to give up or request a dissolution. Such relationships can often be saved if the underlying issues are addressed. Stop entertaining the thought that it was a big mistake for the two of you to have gotten married in the first place. There is still a huge possibility of rediscovering yourselves and finding out how you are a match for each other. Divorce or remarriage are not always the best solutions. The hurt occasioned by a divorce is sometimes as deep as that occasioned by a spouse's death. Therefore, when the danger signs of divorce are beckoning, we should work extra hard to avoid it. When both **communication and sharing a common bedroom have been stopped, the cessation of intimacy and sexual expression will be next—a red zone area that precedes dissolution.**

Unless we exercise the **gift of forgiveness**, which takes away the burden of resentment and loathing from us, how else are we going to operate in a healthy marriage relationship? We are all prone to mistakes and hurts here and there, and this is expected of people who are in long-term relationships. Paul cautions us not to count wrongs or keep a record of them. That doesn't help but increases the possibility of developing complicated diseases like blood pressure and diabetes. Learn to forgive and move on. Remember, a relationship that is filled with strife and discord does not mirror the model of Christ and the Church, and for that reason, your prayers will be hindered. The Apostle Peter says, "Husbands, likewise, dwell with them with understanding, giving honor to the wife, as to the weaker vessel, and as being heirs together of the grace of life, that your prayers may not be hindered" (1 Peter 3:7 [NKJV]). Husbands have a greater responsibility to ensure that peace and harmony remain the hallmarks of their marriage relationship.

Another weapon the devil uses to extinguish the spark is bombarding a couple with the spirit of **doubt.** After some time of being in a relationship, some unsavory questions start making rounds in our minds, "Does my husband/wife love me still?" "Does s/he stand by our marriage vows?" and so on. Because, as humans, we are given to forgetting, we should not leave the void to be filled with doubt, but **from time to time, remind our spouses that we love them** and that they are everything to us. Look for a good time to give this important reminder and whenever possible, accompany those therapeutic words with a **fancy little keepsake for your sweetheart. Affirming and validating** your spouse keeps a tottering relationship from collapsing. Bear in mind that husbands and wives alike want this assurance and validation because we all fall victim to doubt.

Going out for a vacation with your spouse often rekindles the embers of your first love and reignites the spark. The more you invest in a marriage, the more it will give back. If you invest more love, you will reap more love in return, and vice versa. Being in the same location sometimes breeds boredom, in which case taking time away from the routine scene creates the opportunity to see new sights and even think differently. The novelty of a new environment stimulates new worldviews and a fresh way of looking at things. Outings create windows to appreciate what nature has offered to make our lives great. This kind of positive thinking is likely to spill over into our marriages while we vacation with our better halves. After such outings, the negative energy is all consumed, making it possible for a new start with positive energy.

Partners need to exhibit a high sense of **integrity and trustworthiness** to each other. When a spouse feels you are not trustworthy, insecurity and uncertainty set into the relationship. Queries arise as to whether the marriage vows will be upheld if trust and integrity are questionable. Lack of trust and integrity lead to low self-esteem, as one spouse may feel they are not considered important if the other plays the untrustworthy and lack of integrity card. Not fulfilling promises eats into the core of the marriage and undermines the trust that should undergird it. When trust flounders or is lost in a marriage relationship, it remains like a dry husk without the sap that gives it vitality. In an ideal situation, spouses should trust each other to death. If you cannot trust your spouse, who else can you trust? Lack of trust and integrity effectively erodes any traces of love that keep a marriage alive and kicking.

More importantly, the most valuable weapon that all couples must seek to be armed with is getting a handle on how disputes and arguments are resolved in a manner that adds to the marriage's good health. Needless to say, with every couple, no matter how agreeable they look, there comes a time when they disagree, and the tone of their speech, words, and body language all point to two people with contrasting opinions of the same thing. When a disagreement is not nipped in the bud early enough, it degenerates into an argument. In an argument, like in any other fight, each party wants to win by blaming the other or getting defensive. If the argument is allowed to escalate, the partners negatively respond to each other in anger and frustration. When arguments escalate out of control, they amount to a fight where words inflict pain, as would physical weapons. The wounds caused sometimes take a long time to heal, while some don't get healed at all. It is important that instead of engaging in such unproductive arguments, we learn how to change the course of a negative argument into a positive one, which can make the relationship move forward. This **communication skill** is key to putting a cyclic blame and counter blame game to an end. How to get out of a negative argument is the greatest challenge many marriage relationships are faced with today. Let's examine some of the communication approaches taken to deal with arguments between couples.

Giving in: This technique involves throwing in the towel in order to stop arguing. This kind of resolution is unhealthy because the one who ceases to argue is seen as the loser, while the other is seen as the winner. This may temporarily stop the fighting, but a dangerous build-up of resentment and rage continues inside of the apparent loser, which can explode like a volcano at any time in the future with just a little provocation. It is also unhealthy because, apart from the problem not being solved, the one who yielded is likely to develop depression and resentment toward the other one.

Escapism: This is the case when you feel you are at a loss in figuring out the problem with the marriage, and you spend the time and energy you would have taken to solve the problem on another thing instead. This is the time many spouses engage in infidelity or excessive drinking as a defense mechanism to shed their frustration. Others who may not find infidelity or drinking better outlets to vent their frustration may turn to something positive, like working out for long hours at the gym or even working for long hours on an antique project in the garage. I once found a minister colleague who told me his marriage had come under a very vicious attack. He could not understand the origin of his wife's incessant nagging that had turned their previously wonderful home into a toxic and stuffy battleground. He told me that he was experiencing severe depression and decided to take a sabbatical to write a book. Whereas couples may come up with different defense mechanisms to cope with an emotionally draining situation like this one, it is advised that, during such, you should look for professional marriage therapists or counselors to help you. Quite often, hope will be within reach, and the marriage can bounce back with a new lease on life.

Avoidance: This happens when you avoid talking about the problem. This is a deliberate avoidance of discussing the problem by either walking away or avoiding engaging in the topic by simply keeping silent. The avoidance is extended to phone calls, text messages, or emissaries or proxies that might be sent by one of the partners to broker dialogue. When communication is severed, there is usually a build-up of ice between the two, which leads to uncertainty and often depression. The partners feel worlds apart, indicative of the resultant emotional and social distance between the husband and the wife. If severance in communication is allowed to go on for a long time, the marriage might not survive, as the emotional distance will create room for extreme resentment, hate, and vengeance. In extreme cases, some spouses wish for the death of their better halves! That shows how things can get out of hand when grandstanding juts its ugly head into a marriage relationship. Remember, all these meltdowns could otherwise not happen if couples embrace the spirit of forgiveness and shun the vain glory of competing at the expense of greater ideals of life.

Attacking to win: There are certain fights where bitter arguments persist, with each wanting to win the fight by accusing the other of being responsible for the problems they are experiencing in the marriage. No one accepts blame, each bursting out with anger directed at the other until a compromise is reached, where one of them is taken as the winner, and the other is declared the loser. Such settlement is unhealthy because the one who is beaten to submission will harbor a grudge and develop resentment leading to depression and other related emotional breakdowns if not addressed.

Compromise*:* This is the best and healthiest conflict resolution formula. It involves listening to each other's grievances, appreciating them, and seeking the best ways they can be reasonably resolved. The resolution may involve shifting grounds and finding an amiable compromise that will put an end to the bickering. Therefore, the resolution is mutually constructed by finding an acceptable median for the interlocutors' two extreme positions. Because the complaints raised on each side are carefully investigated, and a way forward is arrived at, the couples emerge stronger in a compromising settlement. Such a settlement guarantees a peaceful and harmonious relationship. Remember, all women need a person who will respect their opinions and appreciate them. If a husband cannot understand that, they are likely to have unending squabbles, and, in the worst-case scenario, when women can't find appreciation and validation from their own husbands, they get tempted to look for it elsewhere. Therefore, a balanced resolution in a marital fight will always make the struggling marriage roll back with gusto and vibrance. The relationship becomes new, and the bond of love becomes much stronger.

Chapter Eight:
DEALING WITH ANGER
IN YOUR MARRIAGE

A nger is an emotion just like love or hate, but anger could further be classified as a secondary emotion because it is a sign of a distasteful or detestable underlying primary emotion. For instance, a wife may say she is angry because her husband comes home late and, therefore, she feels unloved by him. The primary emotion, in this case, is the feeling of being unloved by her husband. This is the emotion that triggers anger in this lady. Therefore, we can say that anger is a manifestation of a deeper problem. To resolve the anger issue effectively, we must track it down to its underlying pain or cause of discomfort. Until that is addressed, any other efforts to resolve the anger that causes the ensuing fight will be an exercise in futility. Some causes of anger could be fears or experiences that form the baggage from our family of origin. If one or both spouses grew up in homes where the parents were always fighting and expressing fits of anger, then as children, the spouses could have been affected by emotional disorders like anxiety which could be disturbing their own marriage. In a situation like that, a professional counselor or therapist comes in handy to unwind those terrible experiences from their minds, so they can live happy and harmonious lives. Up until those steps are taken, there may be an insignificant resolution of the anger crisis.

Therefore, while anger is an emotion inherent in all humans, it is its expression that counts as to whether it is expressed healthily. Excessive and misplaced anger is the greatest single killer of marriage relationships in the world.

Anger predisposes its victims to heart attacks, blood pressure surges, depression, impaired immune systems, and other complicated health conditions. Worse still, cases of spouses that have been murdered through fits of anger run to many millions. While some of the causes of being prone to fits of anger and rage could be traced to an individual's family of origin, other causes include emotional and psychotic disorders such as Bipolar disorder, PTSD, and Schizophrenia. If a child grows up in a home where parents fight from time to time, they will develop emotional disturbances, which will replicate later in their lives once they themselves get married. For this reason, children with a background of divorced parents are at a higher risk of divorce once they grow up and get married than children who grew up in a home where their parents lived in peace and never divorced. It is of great importance that parents live in peace and harmony in order not to affect the emotional stability and wellbeing of their children. Let's start by looking at what the scripture says about anger, its expression, and its effects on family members.

The scripture in Proverbs15:1-2 [NIV] says, "A gentle answer turns away wrath, but a harsh word stirs up anger. The tongue of the wise adorns knowledge, but the mouth of a fool gushes folly." Solomon, the pinnacle of the world's wise humans, says in the first verse that the remedy for anger, however great it may be, is a sweet answer. Anger, once expressed, should be responded to by a sweet answer. A sweet answer repulses wrath, but a foul answer that causes vexation causes anger to rise even higher. The Bible in 1 Samuel 25:1-34 tells of an incident where David and his six hundred warriors were hiding in the Desert of Paran to escape the indignation of Saul, who was looking to take his life because he knew he had been anointed to become King over Israel. As David pitched camp in the wilderness with his soldiers, they met and helped the shepherds of a wealthy man called Nabal, whose wife was called Abigail. Nabal was mean-spirited in all his dealings, but his wife was intelligent and beautiful.

When the time for shearing the sheep came, David sent his soldiers with a message to request Nabal to give them any supplies he had because they never harmed his shepherds but protected and helped them while they grazed their flocks in the wilderness of Paran. But Nabal, being mean and foolish as his name implied, sent away David's soldiers empty-handed and even insulted them, saying, "Who is this David? Who is this son of Jesse? Many servants are breaking away from their masters these days. Why should I take my bread and water, and meat I have slaughtered for my shearers, and give them to men coming from who knows where?" (vv 10-11).

When the soldiers reported back to David, he was very angry and told about 400 soldiers to bear up their arms so they could raid and destroy the ungrateful foolish rich man. As they were heading there, David said, "It has been useless – all my watching over this fellow's property in the wilderness so that nothing of his was missing. He has paid me back evil for good. May God deal with David be it ever so severely, if by morning I leave alive one male of all who belong to him" (vv 21-22).

As David was preparing for the raid, Nabal's servants had a premonition of the impending attack and quickly briefed his wife, Abigail. She quickly packed many assorted food items, loaded them onto her donkeys, and instructed her servants to go ahead of her and take them to David and his men as she followed them from behind. On their way, they met David and his men; Abigail quickly disembarked from her donkey and bowed down before him with her face to the ground. She fell on her feet and said, "Pardon your servant my lord, and let me speak to you; hear what your servant has to say. Please pay no attention, my lord, to that wicked man Nabal. He is just like his name—his name means Fool, and folly goes with him. And as for me, your servant, I did not see the men my lord sent" (vv 24-25).

Abigail then implored David to accept the gifts she had brought him and his soldiers. She added, "please forgive your servant's presumption. The Lord your God will certainly make a lasting dynasty for my lord, because you fight the Lord's battles and no wrongdoing will be found in you as long as you live" (vv 28).

David listened to Abigail's words and repented of his anger, saying, "...as surely as the Lord, the God of Israel, lives, who has kept me from harming you, if you had not come quickly to meet me, not one male belonging to Nabal would have been left alive by daybreak.' Then David accepted from her hand what she had brought him and said, 'Go home in peace. I have heard your words and granted your request" (vv 34-35).

The previous story illustrates how humble and kind words can neutralize even extreme anger. See how David came breathing fire, but before he could wreak havoc on the belligerent and foolish Nabal, Abigail stands in the gap to take full responsibility for the foolish and mean behavior of her husband; she apologizes profusely and presents David with an array of food. Her wise, prompt, persuasive, and kind words avert what could have otherwise been a major catastrophe. Therefore, the best way of dealing with destructive anger is to respond with kind and apologetic words. If someone directs their anger on you, you don't have to respond with anger as well.

The Scripture in James 1:19-20 says, "My dear brothers and sisters, take note of this: Everyone should be quick to listen, slow to speak and slow to become angry, because human anger does not produce the righteousness that God desires." "Quick to listen" is an important first step toward resolving an expression of excessive anger. When confronted with an agitated person or spouse who is seething with rage, the best and only biblical response is to listen carefully and not interrupt their rants. That will make them feel respected as their sentiments or complaints get considered. That will deescalate the anger. Angry people will get angrier if they find no one is listening to the cause of their resentment, but once someone pays careful attention, the anger abates. Therefore, James exhorts and cautions the believers in his ministry and the ministry of the Lord worldwide that the best way of countering misplaced or excessive anger is not by seething an equal amount of rage but by just keeping quiet and listening.

"Slow to speak" is an important biblical principle that ensures that we give the other party all the time they need to express their anger so they may feel heard. That is an important step towards healing. Many of those who yell and rant against their spouses do so because they feel their complaints have been ignored, no one has bothered to listen to them, yet they are hurting. Moreover, being listened to sets the assurance that a remedy will be put in place and put an end to the underlying hurt which causes the fighting. Also, being slow to speak gives the angry party an opportunity to unload and vent out their baggage which leads to a release from the tenterhooks of their venomous anger. In conclusion, if someone asks you the best response for a person expressing anger through rants and tirades, the answer is attentive listening with little or no speech, depending on the circumstances.

Finally, when confronted with an angry person or, in our context, an angry spouse, we should not let our emotions get stirred to the extent of shouting back in rage. In those circumstances, the best response is to keep our cool and only respond when the quarreling party has cooled their temper and allowed reason to take over. A dialogue at that stage is more likely to be productive and healthy to move the relationship forward. When anger is spewed out at you, just receive it but don't throw it back to the sender. Just keep your cool and help the agitated party sober up and let reason take over. That is what scripture means when it says to be slow to get angry. When we allow ourselves to be actively angry at each other in a relationship, the environment becomes unlivable, toxic, and obnoxious. I guess nothing could be more boring than being in an atmosphere where spouses are throwing barbs at each other because of anger and resentment.

Also, it should be noted that anger as an emotion is a complex subject that has roped in input from thousands of theorists and researchers over the years. So much has been said, but still, millions upon millions of couples struggle to tame the destructive expression of anger. Whereas the scriptures give guidelines on how to navigate through anger successfully, let's remember at the back of our minds that a soft word or even not speaking at all is a great starting point to confront the fire of anger. Among the Kisii of Western Kenya, the old women used to train younger women how to reign in their anger to avoid nasty outbursts and fights with their husbands. The older mamas taught that whenever a wife saw her husband menacingly confronting her with fits of rage and outbursts, she should sip lots of water and keep it within her mouth without swallowing it. The water should be kept inside the mouth to keep her from responding to her angry husband.

That method worked for them most of the time, but for a few incidents, like one where a wife held a mouthful of water within her cheeks, but her drunken husband thought that was a license to continue hurling violent words at her ad infinitum. Soon, she couldn't stand the bombardment anymore, so she quickly swallowed the water in her mouth and screamed as she ran out of the house, hurling expletives directed at her husband at the top of her lungs. He was hot on her heels even as she sought refuge in a neighbor's house. Of course, that was a traditional technique that should be classified as obsolete because it placed the burden of anger control upon wives while their husbands were exempt and had a license to run amok at will, and everybody would be petrified because the lion was roaring.

Nonetheless, holding water in the mouth could work for some; for others, it was a tall order because silence doesn't diffuse any anger, and that runs the danger of bursting out, as in the above couple's case. However, verbalizing with kind and persuasive words may work best, as it releases the tension in the respondent, while the kind words could disarm the aggressor.

Chapter Nine:
DIVORCE PROOFING YOUR MARRIAGE

D ivorce is a negative word, just like death, bankruptcy, cancer, starvation, or defeat. Do not entertain negative thoughts that represent negative phenomena such as divorce or death to appear as though they are good and beneficial. Those are deceptive thoughts that should be banished from our minds, so we may have the right attitudes and perspectives about life. The bubble of marriage is meant to be floating for as long as we remain true to our marriage vows. It needs protection from headwinds in all directions because it is vulnerable and fragile. Left unprotected, the bubble will soon come down, ruptured and tottering in different directions. For this reason, those who know the immeasurable value of their marriage will stop at nothing to make sure it blossoms and blisses with a glow more precious than gold.

As pointed out in the previous chapters, to make a marriage work out is to avoid quarreling and yelling at one another as much as you can. It feels nasty and degrading to reach that point. Before arguments can degenerate into verbal and emotional abuse, you should practice listening to each other's complaints without interruption. As indicated above, the best response to a complaint is to accept the mistake and take full responsibility. Avoid getting defensive at all costs because it heightens the tension that leads to contempt and disparaging remarks like, "I don't know how I came to be with you, and we ended up being a couple." The other one might retort back, "I regret that day, too." Once a relationship has degenerated to that level, where contempt is openly displayed through negative words, body language, and gestures, the relationship is headed to dissolution and divorce.

Remember when, for some reason, it happens that a marriage that was once so vibrant doesn't emit its characteristic glow anymore? It is then time to double-check whether all the cogs of the relationship are running right. Are they squeaky and need greasing? The cogs of honesty, trust, forgiveness, empathy, validation, sharing emotions, affirmation, worshipping together, playing together, and eating together, if running optimally, may work towards fool-proofing a marriage against divorce. We shall examine each of them in turn to appreciate their primacy in forging unbreakable bonds in marriage.

TRUST: The foundation of trust in marriage is believing in the Lord Jesus Christ as a couple and as individuals in the commonwealth of faith. Once you both trust in the Lord, trusting each other won't be a problem. In a marriage relationship, couples must learn to trust and be trusted more than anything else. A healthy relationship can never be realized if devoid of mutual trust between couples. Trust is the litmus test that ascertains whether a marriage relationship is authentic or pseudo. In Proverbs 31:11 [NKJV], the scripture says, "The heart of her husband safely trusts in her; So he will have no lack of gain." Whereas this portion of scripture underscores the centrality of trust in a marital relationship, King Lemuel gives us a clear signal that we must inspire our spouses' trust. If we conduct ourselves in ways that make it difficult for others to deposit their trust in us, it then follows that they won't trust us. In other words, trust is not a spontaneous reaction but something that we have to inculcate over time, failure to which we shall remain untrustworthy.

Once trust is injured, it may take some time before the wounds can heal. Some hurts may be so deep that their healing may take ages to come about, and even after they have healed, lifelong scars remain. This reminds us how important it is in a relationship to keep our integrity and trust beyond reproach. It is a very low moment when a spouse tells a lie to the other or does anything that puts their trust into question. When there is trust in a relationship, the need to snoop into your partner's cell phone text messages won't arise because you trust them.

SHARING EMOTIONS: Nothing makes a relationship more authentic than sharing our struggles as well as our triumphs. When a couple stands shoulder to shoulder through a difficult moment, they bond and become very strong. Celebrating together has a similar effect. Imagine one partner celebrating their birthday while the other is seemingly uninterested or uninvolved and how weird it would look. Sharing moments when emotions are high has the capacity to draw us closer to each other than would be the case in normal circumstances. If you are attending a public event as a couple and suddenly emotions start running high, that is the time to stand together and offer support to the vulnerable one. Support coming at such times leaves an indelible imprint in the heart of the one who received it. It is not prudent to delegate such an important function to anybody else because of the spontaneous bonding that takes place. Emotionally demanding occasions draw from the soul and are why, at times, the one offering the emotional support may develop an intimate relationship with the one being supported, especially if the emotions are deep and run for a longer period.

EMPATHY: Can be said to be the ability to understand another person's feelings (while *sympathy* means sharing in the feelings of another person). It is emotionally tragic to take each other for granted or assume they can cope with what life gives them without necessarily requiring input from our end. Couples are essentially helpmates physically, emotionally, socially, and spiritually. That is what God had in mind when he said, "...It is not good that the man should be alone; I will make him an help meet for him" (Genesis 2:18 [KJV]). Empathy transcends the mind and the heart, reaching out to the soul. The soul is the innermost self, the very essence of the psyche on which God bestowed the work of his creation. Therefore, empathy is not just an ordinary feeling or attitude we develop towards a person in pain but a deeper emotional connection that reverberates between two individuals.

When a couple is disjointed and lives two parallel lives, it is hard for either to look at a situation through the lens of the other. It is for that reason an emotional connection capable of eliciting empathy may be difficult to achieve. Therefore, when couples feel distant, they should focus on each other's strong points and stop focusing on the weak or negative points. Think of something you appreciate about your partner and focus on it. This will help to bridge the distance and create empathy. Make room in your heart for your spouse. Think about what they are struggling with and pray for them.

Another way of emotionally drawing close to your spouse is by getting interested in how they are feeling. Taking time to get to know your better half's feelings will trigger a soul connection between you. It is kind of selfish when we only care about our feelings and take our partner's feelings for granted. When we get to the nitty-gritty of how our partners feel, we make them feel loved by us, and emotional bonds emerge, including empathy for when we are in pain or in awkward fixes. Understanding another person's feelings takes time, patience, and careful attention. We must be ready to sacrifice all of those for the sake of our better halves so we can make them feel loved and taken care of by us.

HONESTY: This is the capacity to be truthful in your dealings with others. If you ask prospective partners what qualities they would like to have in their relationships, many will mention honesty. When you trust your spouse, it makes you feel secure and removes the burden of worry from your relationship. Security and lack of worry are basic needs, which, once met, give a general feeling that life is good. Having a spouse you cannot trust because they are dishonest will make you unsteady and erratic, both in your thought process and actions. This is because you experience insecurity, which may result in panic attacks as your emotional environment is not stable. A dishonest mate can cause you to feel inadequate and unlucky. In short, dishonesty in marriage is a debilitating disability.

Some people argue that it is impossible to tell your spouse 100% truth all the time and that some truths may hurt your spouse. Much as that could be true, it is important to remember that telling lies or half-truths can completely damage your relationship beyond repair. When the tongue gets used to coating lies to look true, it becomes a dangerous tool to possess because it can come up with a whole world of falsehoods that can be very embarrassing to identify with.

A spouse may have some cash in their accounts that they want to keep from their partner, and, therefore, they tell a lie to hide the truth about the money. However, if someone has agreed to share their lives with you and to open their hearts so that you know what is inside, isn't it an act of destructive selfishness to lie about the cash in our bank accounts? The Scripture says, "A lying tongue hates those it hurts, and a flattering mouth works ruin" (Proverbs 26:28 [NIV]).

FORGIVENESS: When you feel disappointed, angry, or betrayed by your spouse, forgiving them feels like an uphill task because, to you, it feels like letting them get away with it. You feel that to get even, you must be distant, gloomy, and sulky. Such feelings are normal, but we must get out of the vicious cycle of revenge to get a release from the emotional hurt such feelings engender. Forgiveness is a deliberate step to let go of all the pain, hurt, and resentment to start a new chapter as though nothing bad had happened. It is a deliberate surrender of the right to revenge or to retaliate against someone who has hurt you. Forgiving does not necessarily mean forgetting the wrong or injury but letting go of any malice or ill intention that you may be harboring against those who wronged or hurt you.

In a marriage relationship, it is not going to be rosy all the time. Times will come when you find that your spouse has inadvertently or purposely stepped on your toes. The best response in a situation like that is not hitting back or stepping on their toes to get even, but instead exercising the restraint to not answer a wrong with a wrong. Paul, writing to caution those bent on avenging any evils done to them in the church in Rome, says, "Do not repay anyone evil for evil. Be careful to do what is right in the eyes of everyone. If it is possible, as far as it depends on you, live at peace with everyone. Do not take revenge, my dear friends, but leave room for God's wrath, for it is written: 'It is mine to revenge; I will repay,' says the Lord. On the contrary: 'if your enemy is hungry, feed him; if he is thirsty, give him something to drink. In doing this, you will heap burning coals on his head.' Do not be overcome with evil, but overcome evil with good" (Romans 12:17-21 [NIV]). Revenge is not as effective as laying burning coals on your adversary's head by being good to them, even when they have been demeaning and hurtful. I try it most of the time, and I feel satisfied and vindicated.

Forgiveness is healthy for a marriage relationship and the offended person. A relationship worked out on a platform of unforgiveness is dysfunctional, unhealthy, and untenable.

Some have said that marriage is a partnership between two good forgivers. Forgiveness helps the aggrieved person shed off the baggage of resentment and hate, which could otherwise cause untold emotional and psychological damage and overall body wellness. When expressing unconditional forgiveness, it is better for a spouse to explain to the other how their behavior, statement, or in/action hurt them, so they can know a better way of going about it next time. An act of forgiveness reinvigorates a marriage relationship and boosts self-esteem as you get the certainty that you are following God's way.

VALIDATION: This is a great thing to do to strengthen intimacy in a relationship. It is emotionally giving a thumbs up to your better half even if you don't necessarily believe in what they say. It is an unconditional approval of your spouse's position to show that you value their heart and emotions, regardless of whether they make sense or not. To validate means to support and agree with an idea, thought, opinion, belief, feeling, or debate advanced by your spouse.

Sandra and her husband, Jim, attend their end-of-year neighborhood's association meeting, where the attendees resolve to elect their new chairperson. Jim expresses interest in the position even though most of the members want to retain the current chairman, whose performance has been extraordinary. The convener gives out ballots and requests all those in attendance to cast a vote between the incumbent, Mr. Warren, and Jim to elect their new chairperson. Meanwhile, Warren and Jim are asked to cast their ballots first and go to the next room as the rest of the members cast theirs too.

Once the ballots are counted, Warren wins almost all the votes, and Jim gets only his own vote. Jim feels quite embarrassed that he only got his own vote, but what disturbs him even more is that his wife, Sandra, did not vote for him. As Jim sits next to his wife, his disappointment is obvious to everybody in the room. Jim mumbles as he positions himself on the couch, "What happened, honey, that I couldn't even get your consoling vote?" Sandra says, "Honey, I think Warren is a better chairperson, and he deserves a unanimous vote. Sorry about it, but I didn't intend to hurt you." Jim says, "It is Okay," with his head facing down in a pensive mood.

In the above incident, Sandra behaved in a hurtful way that invalidated her husband, Jim, instead of supporting him. Invalidation is the last thing a married couple should do to each other, especially in public. Such hurts may be unintentional, but, as Sandra says, they can take a long time, perhaps as long as a lifetime, to heal. Again, validation means unconditional support or acceptance of your spouse's position, even if you don't believe it is the correct position.

PRAYING TOGETHER: The saying, "A family that prays together stays together," can't be overemphasized. Key findings from new major research on minority families done by sociologist W. Bradford Wilcox indicate that the couple that prays together actually does stay together, statistically speaking.[20] As revealed through an investigation

---

[20] Morgan Lee, Interviewer, "The Data Don't Lie: Couples that Pray Together Actually Do Stay Together," *Christianity Today*, christinaityto-day.com (March 18, 2016), https://www.christinaitytoday.com/ct/2016/april/data-don't-lie-couples-that-pray-together-actually-do=stay-t.html

carried out by Professor Wilcox on a low-income minority population living in the New York City suburbs. He discovered that Christ-believing and born-again families had the lowest numbers of marriage dissolutions. When you pray together, it creates an air of piety that ignites a consciousness of your obligation to fear God by observing marriage vows and covenant faithfulness. Prayer keeps the Spirit of God at work in you, which minimizes the possibility of falling into temptations of infidelity and hurting each other's feelings. Praying together makes God's presence encompass and protect you. In God's presence, as scripture says, there is fullness of joy. That is why couples who pray together are always joyful and happy.

Praying together encourages intimacy and trust in a relationship. A couple that becomes prayer-mates connects emotionally and spiritually at a much deeper level, touching their souls. Such a strong bond can withstand storms that knock down prayerless marriage relationships or those who pray separately. It has been said that when a husband and wife pray separately, many things happen, but when they pray together, tremendous things happen, much more than when they pray individually.

Praying together helps couples understand each other better as they mention each other's weaknesses and struggles before the living God. Feelings of empathy and vulnerability get evoked during joint devotions, which helps to strengthen the marriage. Truly, couples who pray together are blessed. Nothing draws couples together more than an act of praying together. When all of my six older children were young and living with me, whenever we had a serious threat facing the family, I explained it to them while holding our hands together, and I requested each one of us, including their mother, take turns and pray for the problem, while the rest listened or interjected in affirmation with "Amen! Yes, Lord! Hallelujah!" I cannot remember a single time when God didn't intervene or answer our prayers. When we unite and join our spirits into one accord, God can never fail to honor and respond to our petitions.

Chapter Ten:
SEXUALITY AND INFIDELITY

E very community has clear guidelines that inform the expression of human sexuality. Sex ethics are an integral aspect of not only Christian ethics but also of any ethical system. This is an area that is wont to be misused in the absence of effective structures to direct its use. Yet, its centrality for procreation, mutual fulfillment, and enjoyment within ethically permissible parameters can never be overemphasized. Whereas sex cannot be enjoyed like we do when eating, say, a candy bar or chocolate, we need to give it its distinctive God-given place in life. Let's look at a few topical and salient issues that should serve as a guideline in the ethical use of this amazing God-given resource.

Most communities advocate for abstinence from sexual intercourse until the appropriate age is attained and preparations for receiving it promulgated. Sex must be received within the context of a covenant involving a mutual agreement between the participants and their ethical society. Outside of the accepted boundaries, sex becomes fornication or adultery. Jesus' teaching on sex emphasized a rigorous discipline that forbids not only the act but also even the mere imagination of it (Matthew 5:27-30 [ESV]). The Old Testament law also forbade sex outside of marriage (Exodus 20:14 [ESV]).

Sexual intercourse outside of marriage risks the conception of children, and children born outside of marriage are more likely to be emotionally deprived, neglected, or hindered. That is the reason it was regulated by norms and values governing most Old Testament communities.

On the other hand, infidelity or cheating refers to a breach of the commitment to sexual exclusivity. Cheating usually happens on the back of the committed partner and may take several forms, including sex, fondling, flirting beyond expected limits, kissing, caressing, emotional connections that are beyond friendships, internet relationships (e.g., through Facebook, Skype, WhatsApp, Instagram, etc.), viewing pornographic material, and many more. The biblical or theological terms for infidelity include unfaithfulness, immorality, adultery, etc. What constitutes an act of infidelity varies according to cultural norms and the type of relationship between the two people, but the loathe and stigma associated with it cut across the divide. Whether the act of infidelity involving a relationship partner takes a few minutes or a one-night stand with a work colleague out on official duty, the trust and faithfulness that undergirds the commitment to a relationship has been violated and will never be the same again. The trauma and injuries involving the violation of trust through infidelity in intimate relationships have been known to sometimes last for a lifetime.

The subject of infidelity is getting complex. More and more research needs to be carried out to keep pace with its mutating form and nature. The traditional infidelity that involved two people having physical contact has since been overtaken by internet infidelity, where the partners could be thousands of miles apart but still have a clandestine, emotionally captivating, and tantalizing relationship. An unsuspecting partner could be in their bed sleeping while the other unfaithful one could be chatting and sexting with an internet lover in another continent on their muted smartphones. That is how complex this issue has become. It is noteworthy that any form of investment in sexuality outside of the exclusivity of marriage is infidelity.

With the rate of divorce on a rising trajectory in the United States, so are cheating and infidelity in relationships. The last twenty-five years have seen a sharp rise in cheating cases in the U.S. Surveys show that most women cheat, not because they need sex but because they need an emotional connection. When women are not satisfied emotionally, they initiate an affair with some other person they trust, just for the sake of love. Some, longing to get validation or affirmation, which may not be coming from their husbands, look for it elsewhere through infidelity. On the other hand, most men cheat for a single primary reason, sex.[21]

The statistics available for infidelity are troubling, to say the least. While 90 percent of Americans believe it is morally wrong to commit an adulterous act, only 61 percent would

[21] "Latest Infidelity Statistics of USA," Divorce statistics , https://www.divorcestatistics.info/latest-infidelity-statistics-of-usa.html

like to see it being punished like any other crime. It is estimated that about 22 percent of married men have cheated on their wives at least once in their lifetime, while 14 percent of women have had an affair at least once during their married life. More data shows that 36 percent of men and women admit to having affairs with co-workers, with whom they spend more time than their spouses. Another 36 percent of men and women admit to having had an affair during a business trip. And 2 percent to 3 percent of all the children are a result of infidelity relationships and are unknowingly raised by men who are not their biological fathers.[22]

The above information and numbers are an overview of what is taking place across the landscape; let us now narrow the topic to what the scripture says about infidelity. The Old Testament teaching on covenant fidelity in marriage is addressed in multiple chapters, either directly or symbolically. God decries Israel's infidelity to her covenant with him through the metaphor of Hosea's promiscuous wife. God directed the prophet to marry her, her immoral character notwithstanding, so he could have a handle on what He was going through in his covenant relationship with immoral Israel (Hosea1:2, 2:2, [ESV]). Moral commands in the Old Testament and New Testament both enjoin exclusivity of the marriage bed in order to have a trusting, loyal, mutually affirming, problem-overcoming, and alienation-healing covenant bond.[23]

---

[22] Anderson, K. G, (2006). How well does paternity confidence match actual paternity? Evidence from worldwide nonpaternity rates. *Current Anthropology 48, in press.*

[23] Stassen, H. Glen and David P. Gushee. *Kingdom Ethics: Following Jesus in Contemporary Context.* Downers Grove, Intervarsity Press, 2003.

In the New Testament, Paul warns the Church in the port city of Corinth because they had not cut off links with Temple prostitution in the worship of Aphrodite, the goddess of beauty. This business hub was famous for sexual immorality. Paul warns, "Flee from sexual immorality. All other sins a person commits are outside the body, but whoever sins sexually, sins against their own body" (1 Corinthians 6:18 [NIV]). The choice of the apostle's words tells it all. To "flee" gives the sense of running away from danger. The word brings out the urgency that should be attached to that action, explaining how dangerous infidelity is to those who engage in it. In his epistle to Timothy, he uses the same word, exhorting, "So flee youthful passions and pursue righteousness, faith, love, and peace, along with those who call on the Lord from a pure heart" (2 Timothy 2:22 [ESV]).

Jesus was even more emphatic; he warned that if a person looks at a woman lustfully, he has already committed adultery with her in his heart (Matthew 5:28 [NIV]). So, the Lord Jesus Christ raised the bar on infidelity up to the level where even a lustful desire of the eyes without any physical contact is considered the same as one involving bodily contact. This means those who take sexual immorality for granted are on their path to self-destruction. Infidelity is so destructive that its damage has effects that may span a lifetime and beyond. Even children born of adulterous relationships suffer low esteem and other emotionally related problems.

Quite often, long before a person in a marriage relationship makes advances to a paramour for a sexual favor, secret admiration propelled by lust has taken place in the mind and the heart. Unless lust is exhaustively dealt with and eliminated in a person's life, it is not possible to experience victorious Christian living. Unaided humans are controlled by the flesh and apt to indulge in a perverted use of sex. Getting delivered from the lust of the eyes is a major milestone for whoever wants to live honorable married lives before the Lord.

Some people have struggled with lust all their lives as a result of not living pure and cleansed lives. In order to succeed, we should take stock of the kind of programs and movies we watch, what kind of music we listen to, what type of friends we associate with, what books and magazines we read, and what kind of talk comes out of our mouths, etc. All those channels carry the potential of polluting our hearts and minds leaving us unable to break loose from the yoke of lust and infidelity.

To avoid the temptation of falling into sexual immorality, couples committed to keeping the vows of their marriages should shun all flirting. It is dangerous to flirt because, even if it is done in a subtle way, its goal is to get attention from the opposite sex. Such a desire is driven by lust. One of the main ways by which our lusts can be satisfied is by flirting. Flirting is behaving in a certain way with the goal of getting attention from the opposite sex, which is not healthy. Flirting is a form of infidelity that may appear harmless but could explode into vigorous sexual activity given a chance. Avoid compromising and tempting situations if you don't want to fall victim to infidelity. It is not advisable to talk for long hours with someone who is not your relationship partner because that may create an unhealthy emotional connection that always ends in infidelity. Why should we walk into temptations instead of fleeing from them? Couple visitations are the best and most secure way of meeting with the opposite sex, especially when the meeting is likely to be long. We must care not only about the danger of playing into the devil's hands but also about the impression and suspicion it could occasion on the onlookers. I trust myself, but I have never felt at ease to give a ride in my truck to a lady unless she is my wife or a close family member. But if I have other passengers in the vehicle, then I have no problem.

Just a reminder to those who have a history of extra-marital affairs, in deciding to be committed and faithful to their spouses come rain or shine, they will discover what they have never known about being married. A marriage whose promises have been broken and vows forsaken is rotten, tasteless, and lackluster. Faithfulness in marriage is priceless and the only way to crack the password that unleashes the mysterious joy and fulfillment embedded in the covenant relationship between husband and wife. Infidelity can be viewed as an emotional disability far more debilitating than any physical handicap which stands in the way of enjoying a fulfilling marital relationship. It eats into the personality and lowers its subjects into becoming victims of low self-esteem.

Chapter Eleven:
UNHEALTHY HABITS
AND PORNOGRAPHY

God created sex so it could be received and enjoyed within strictly regulated circumstances. It was never meant to be a casual encounter or a leisurely activity like you can decide to stand on opposite sides of a court to play ping pong or set wickets to play croquet. On its inception, God gave rules and instructions on how to conduct sex, failure to which the offenders could face God's wrath and judgment in hell for the cardinal sin of committing adultery (Exodus 20:6). Sex has consequences, and it impacts the participants in ways that can be felt throughout their lives. For this reason, only a man and woman who have been joined together as husband and wife should morally engage in sexual intercourse.

Sex is good only when done as per God's prescription and for the intended purposes. It is a blessing to the extent that through it, married couples can multiply and replenish the earth congruent to God's command at Creation. It is also a blessing because when engaging in it, the husband and wife can connect so deeply and intimately that they become "one flesh," an image of the Holy Trinity's unity. It facilitates bonding and neuters icy walls of separation and individualism. The wedding bed is the altar for celebrating the gift of sex, and it must be respected and honored. The respect and honor extend to the linen and all bedding used in the couple's wedding bed. Failure to respect sex is dishonoring God.

Couples must be completely committed and focused on their relationships to maintain a healthy sex life. A spouse who takes their eyes from the focus of their better half will never find the fulfillment that God intended it to elicit. Eyes that wander far and wide, admiring those of the opposite sex, need urgent redemption from lust. Lust is the greatest barrier to celebrating healthy sexual intercourse. The easiest way to overcome lust is first to make a covenant with God that you can NEVER EVER have sex with anyone apart from your married one and only partner. If you make a strong vow not to indulge in sexual impropriety and completely erase any thought that could shift the focus from your spouse, then I believe the demon of lust would have nowhere to hang its dirty linen in your life. When I came to the Lord over thirty years ago, I swore before Him that if I could go back to drinking or indulge in sexual immorality, then he should not allow me to continue living. I have never broken these vows nor lusted after any lady. I believe the demon of lust vacated once it found I was committed to living a Christ-honoring and upright life.

Many people struggle to overcome lust because some doors in their lives remain ajar, and the demon can come in and out at will. One such door is watching films or movies with sexually explicit content. Filter what enters your eyes or your mind. If any garbage readily finds its entry into you, then you are at a big risk of falling prey to lust. Your TV screens should not be used as conduits to pollute your home environments through sexually expressive programs. Filter the music too. Filter the magazines and literature you read to make sure none of it exposes you to the corruption of your morals and probity. Filter even your circle of friends to make sure no door is left ajar. As we said earlier, flirting with a member of the opposite sex arouses lustful desire all the time. To live cleansed and holy lives requires effort; otherwise, we shall be held captive by all manner of spirits.

Some couples fantasize so as to energize their sexual activity when they lose the drive, but that habit should be shunned by all means because it inflicts fatal blows to healthy sex lives. Fantasizing is a product of lust. It is negative, crippling, and debilitating. Anybody who wants to get their full value out of their investment in marriage should make redemption from the spirit of lust a priority; otherwise, it eats into your intimacy, leaving it hollow, superficial, uninteresting, and mechanical. At no time should a spouse allow themselves to think that there is a better partner for them under the sun than the present better half. Concentrate on her/him, for it is the way God intends it to be. **There could be millions of marriageable men and women, but God has set aside only one for you!** Remember, it is only one, not two, three, or even one and a half spouses. Blessed are the eyes that don't wander from perfectly focusing on their better halves.

Since the advent of the smartphone and the internet, one debilitating and perverse online activity has been watching pornographic material. I should think pornography is on the same pedestal as witchcraft, considering how it impacts and controls its captives. Lots of research has been done on pornography to determine its effects on those who are hooked to it, and the results are, to say the least, quite appalling. It is thought that more young adults indulge in pornography than older ones. However, we would like to focus on the effects of pornography on married couples for this primer's purpose.

Watching pornography messes with our emotional state of mind. There are reported cases of low self-esteem, depression, anxiety, and other related psychological disorders in men who are hooked on this perverted activity. Millions of people struggle to get out of its yoke, and just like the case with hard drugs, some get off the hook only to relapse later. Continuous exposure appears to lead to some forms of mental breakdown. The first time I saw pornography was about ten years ago when I had only been in America for two years. I just got strange videos on my laptop and couldn't understand what was happening. I tried to shut down the laptop, but it hung and wouldn't close. I called my wife and asked her to inquire whether our daughters were responsible for visiting the demonic sites on the laptop. They all said they didn't know what was going on. I remember we had a bitter quarrel in our apartment that day. When I later took the laptop for repair, they told me that it had been infected with a virus that was responsible for the porn videos. I went back and apologized to our daughters. However, the sight was powerful, and the shock took weeks to clear out of my mind. Later, I occasionally opened infected folders and found the bizarre pictures, but I quickly closed the files and rebuked their sight in Jesus' name, keeping in mind, it is the second look that causes sin.

Watching explicit sexual content opens the mind to fantasizing, which distorts and overthrows the genuine, realistic, and natural way of perceiving sexuality. Pornography conveys a false meaning and practice of the gift of sexual intimacy as ordained and provided for in the scriptures. Like we have said before, fantasizing is all lust-driven and nothing else. Fantasy and hallucinations share lots of common ground. Of course, I can't trust a hallucinating person to stand behind me with a weapon; they can do anything at any time. Nor can I comfortably leave my newborn in the hands of a hallucinating nanny and go to the store. We can safely conclude that extended pornography viewing leads to mental breakdowns.

Scientific evidence shows that when viewing pornographic content, the excitement is so strong that the brain triggers the production of excess oxytocin, the pleasure-loving hormone, into the bloodstream. Once the body is used to extreme excitement to produce the love hormone, natural or normal sexual intercourse cannot produce enough oxytocin to make the intimacy as fulfilling as God wanted it to be. A couple's sex life may be totally ruined if one of them gets addicted to the fantasy of pornography. To cleanse the mind of the filth of pornography may take quite some time. A therapist or a pastor may help you unlearn the pervasive content and help you keep your mind and thought processes clean.

Moreover, when a partner knows that the other is hooked on watching explicit content, feelings of inadequacy will escalate. A wife is likely to take it personally that the husband doesn't regard her as being up to the task when it comes to lovemaking, which will undermine the marriage's stability a great deal. Statistics have shown that about 500,000 marriages are destroyed annually in the United States because of pornography.[24]

[24] Kevin B. Skinner, "Is Porn Really Destroying 500,000 Marriages Annually?" *Psychology Today*, December 12, 2011, https://www.psychologytoday.com/us/blog/inside-porn-addiction/201112/is-porn-really-destroying-500000-marriages-annually.

REVISION NOTES

Chapter One: DEFINING MARRIAGE

Main Verse: "Therefore shall a man **leave** his father and his mother, and shall **cleave** unto his wife: and they shall be **one flesh**" (Genesis 2:24 [KJV]).

- Marriage must be heterosexual (involving two people of the opposite sex).
- Marriage is essentially a permanent relationship.
- Husband and wife should become "one flesh."
- Marriage is a mirror of Christ and the Church.
- Marriage is meant to be a holy ordinance.

YOUR PERSONAL NOTES

Chapter Two: SUBMISSION AND LOVE

Main Verse: "Wives, submit yourselves unto your own husbands, as unto the Lord" (Ephesians 5:22 [KJV]).

- Submission is not inferiority.
- Submission is a voluntary, selfless yielding to the other in love.
- Submission cannot be reversed or side-stepped as being irrelevant or obsolete.
- Submission brings out the beautiful, feminine characteristic of a wife.
- Submission brings God's blessing into a family based on obedience to the Word.

YOUR PERSONAL NOTES

Chapter Three: HUSBAND AND HEADSHIP

Main Verse: "...instead, the greatest among you shall be like the youngest, and one who rules like the one who serves" (Luke 22:26 [NIV]).

- Headship is not lording it over others.
- Headship is not bossing but anchored on servant-like service/leading.
- Headship is serving, protecting, and providing.
- Headship is taking responsibility for the spiritual welfare of the family and more.

YOUR PERSONAL NOTES

Chapter Four: MARRIAGE AND CHILDREN

Main Verse: "Children are a heritage from the Lord, offspring a reward from him. Like arrows in the hands of a warrior are children born in one's youth. Blessed is the man whose quiver is full of them. They will not be put to shame when they contend with their opponents in court" (Psalms 127: 3-5 [NIV]).

- Children are a blessing from God (Genesis 1:28).
- Children's emotional wellbeing depends on the stability of their family.
- Parents must nurture their children in the admonition of the Lord.
- The children's character is a mirror of the home where they are brought up.

YOUR PERSONAL NOTES

Chapter Five: PARENTING APPROACHES

Main Verse: Train up a child in the way he should go: and when he is old, he will not depart from it (Proverbs 22:6 [KJV]).

- Children have to be loved, treated with respect, and understanding.
- Children's understanding of the nature of God depends on what they perceive of their parents.
- Authoritative parenting is the best approach to bringing up children.
- Christian formation should be attained early in life in their home environment.

YOUR PERSONAL NOTES

Chapter Six: MARRIAGE AND MONEY

Main Verse: "For the love of money is a root of all kinds of evil, for which some have strayed from the faith in their greediness, and pierced themselves through with many sorrows. But you, O man of God, flee these things and pursue righteousness, godliness, faith, love, patience, gentleness" (1 Timothy 6: 10-11 [NKJV]).

- Never put money at the center of your relationship.
- Avoid being spendthrifts and impulse buyers.
- Share financial information freely.
- Put something aside for the winter as much as you can.
- Be good tithers and givers to charity.

YOUR PERSONAL NOTES

Chapter Seven: RESTORING THE FIRST LOVE

Main Verse: "Love is patient, love is kind. It does not envy, it does not boast, it is not proud. It does not dishonor others, it is not self-seeking, it is not easily angered, it keeps no record of wrongs. Love does not delight in evil but rejoices with the truth. It always protects, always trusts, always hopes, always perseveres. Love never fails..." (1 Corinthians 13:4-8 [NIV]).

- Appreciate and validate each other.
- Remind each other that you love them.
- Plan for family vacations.
- Avoid arguments as much as possible.
- Pray together.
- Cherish trust, honesty, and integrity in your marriage.

YOUR PERSONAL NOTES

Chapter Eight: DEALING WITH ANGER IN YOUR MARRIAGE

Main Verse: "A gentle answer turns away wrath, but a harsh word stirs up anger. The tongue of the wise adorns knowledge, but the mouth of a fool gushes folly" (Proverbs15:1-2 [NIV]).

- Anger is a secondary emotion; it has an underlying primary emotion that triggers it.
- Find out the underlying cause of anger and address it.
- Respond with a kind word whenever your spouse hurls misplaced anger – I am sorry, etc.
- Discuss issues when sober and not angry.
- Watch the words you speak; they may cause hurts impossible to heal.

YOUR PERSONAL NOTES

Chapter Nine: DIVORCE PROOFING YOUR MARRIAGE

Main Verse: "The heart of her husband safely trusts in her; So he will have no lack of gain" (Proverbs 31:11 [NKJV]).

- Cease unhealthy arguments and appreciate and honor your spouse.
- Exercise the gift of forgiveness as much as possible.
- Divorce is a negative phenomenon stop fantasizing about it.
- Be humble and submissive to each other.
- Don't dwell on the past; let go, and have a new beginning.

YOUR PERSONAL NOTES

Chapter Ten: SEXUALITY AND INFIDELITY

Main Verse: "Flee from sexual immorality. All other sins a person commits are outside the body, but whoever sins sexually, sins against their own body" (1 Corinthians 6:18 [NIV]).

- Deal with lust exhaustively by cleansing your mind and filtering what goes in and out of you.
- Sexual immorality is degrading yourself.
- Sexual immorality is a scandal not worth the lifelong damage it occasions.
- A spouse who takes their eyes from the focus of their better half will never find the fulfillment that God intended it to elicit.

YOUR PERSONAL NOTES

Chapter Eleven: UNHEALTHY HABITS AND PORNOGRAPHY

Main Verse: "But among you there must not be even a hint of sexual immorality, or of any kind of impurity, or of greed, because these are improper for God's holy people" (Ephesians 5:3 [NIV]).

- Sex has consequences, and it impacts the participants in ways that can be felt throughout their lives.
- Pornography conveys a false meaning and practice of the gift of sexual intimacy as ordained and provided for in the scriptures.
- Watching explicit sexual content opens the mind to fantasizing, which distorts and overthrows the genuine, realistic, and natural way of perceiving sexuality.

YOUR PERSONAL NOTES

BIBLIOGRAPHY

Anderson, K. G. "How Well Does Paternity Confidence Match Actual Paternity?" *Current Anthropology, Vol. 47, No. 3, 2006, pp. 513-520.*

Baumrind, Diana. "Effects of Authoritative Parental Control on Child Behavior." *Child Development*, December 1966, http://persweb.wabash.edu/facstaff/hortonr/articles%20 for%20class/baumrind.pdf.

Bosick, S.J., & Paula Fomby, "Family Instability in Childhood and Criminal Offending During the Transition Into Adulthood." *American Behavioral Scientist*, Vol. 62, No. 11, 2018, pp. 1483 – 1504, https://dol.org/10.1177/0002764218787000

Cherry, Kendra. "Uninvolved Parenting: Characteristics, Effects, and Causes." *Very Well Mind*, July 17, 2019, https://www.verywellmind.com/what-is-uninvolved-parenting-2794958

Christiaensen, Luc. "Domestic violence and poverty in Africa: When the Husband's Beating Stick is Like Butter." *World Bank Blogs*, January 18, 2016, https://blogs.worldbank.org/africacan/domestic-violence-and-poverty-in-africa-when-the-husbands-beating-stick-is-like-butter.

Eller, Vernard. "On Prescription Against Heretics," *The Reincarnation of Quintus Septimius Florens Tertullian.*

Greenberger, Ellen, and Wendy Goldberg. "Work, Parenting, and the Socialization of Children." *Developmental Psychology, Vol. 25*, No. 1, 1989, pp. 22-35, https://doi.org/10.1037/0012-1649.25.1.22.

Grenz, Stanley and Denise Muir Kjesbo. *Women in the Church: A Biblical Theology of Women in Ministry.* Downers Grove, Intervarsity Press, 1995.

Grudem, Wayne. *Evangelical Feminism: A New Path to Liberalism?* Wheaton, Crossway, 2006.

"Latest Infidelity Statistics of USA." *Divorce Statistics Latest Infidelity Statistics of USA Comments.*" www.divorcestatistics.info/latest-infidelity-statistics-of-usa.html.

Lee, Morgan. Interview. "The Data Don't Lie: Couples That Pray Together Actually Do Stay Together.*" Christianity Today*, March 18, 2016, www.christianitytoday.com/ct/2016/april/data-dont-lie-couples-that-pray-together-actually-do-stay-t.html.

"Marriage and Men's Health." *Harvard Health*, July 2010, Updated June 2019, www.health.harvard.edu/mens-health/marriage-and-mens-health.

National marriage and divorce rate trends. PDF File. https://www.cdc.gov/nchs/data/dvs/national-marriage-divorce-rates-00-17.pdf

Piper, John. *What is the Difference: Manhood and Womanhood Defined According to the Bible?* Wheaton, Crossway, 1990.

Piper, John and Wayne Grudem, eds. *Recovering Biblical Manhood and Womanhood: A Response to Evangelical Feminism.* Wheaton, Crossway, 2012.

Russell, Letty M., ed. *The Feminist Interpretation of the Bible.* Philadelphia, Westminster, 1985.

Shaw, Perry W.H. "Parenting that Reflects the Character of God," *Christian Education Journal: Research on Education Ministry,* Series 3, Vol 13, No 1, May 2016, pp. 43-58.

Skinner, Kevin B. "Is Porn Really Destroying 500,000 Marriages Annually." *Psychology Today*, December 12, 2011, https://www.psychologytoday.com/us/blog/inside-porn-addiction/201112/is-porn-really-destroying-500000-marriages-annually.

Stassen, H. Glen and David P. Gushee. *Kingdom Ethics: Following Jesus in Contemporary Context.* Downers Grove, Intervarsity Press, 2003.